THE TEACHING MINISTER

THE TEACHING MINISTER

CLARK M. WILLIAMSON
and
RONALD J. ALLEN

WESTMINSTER / JOHN KNOX PRESS
Louisville, Kentucky

Book design by Publishers' WorkGroup

First edition

Published by Westminster/John Knox Press
Louisville, Kentucky

PRINTED IN THE UNITED STATES OF AMERICA

9 8 7 6 5 4 3 2 1

Library of Congress Cataloging-in-Publication Data

Williamson, Clark M.
   The teaching minister / by Clark M. Williamson and Ronald J.
Allen. — 1st ed.
       p.   cm.
   Includes bibliographical references and index.
   ISBN 0-664-25174-9

   1. Church—Teaching office.   2. Clergy—Office.   3. Tradition
(Theology).   4. Christianity and culture.   5. Protestant churches—
United States—Clergy.   6. United States—Church history—20th
century.   I. Allen, Ronald J. (Ronald James), 1949–   .   II. Title.
BR526.W54   1991
262'.14—dc20   90-46624

CONTENTS

PREFACE

This book addresses a question that is, at once, both one of the oldest and one of the newest, and therefore most critical, questions facing the church today. That question is: What should be the image, model, or role of the clergy? How should Christian pastors understand what the church properly expects and needs from them? What is the central task of the ministry?

That is a question on which it would be easy to waffle; after all, there *are* many important things that ministers are rightly asked to do. In order not to waffle, however, we prefer to state quite plainly that the *central* task of ministry is *teaching* the Christian faith. Preaching itself, for example, is seldom an evangelistic proclamation to a crowd of people who have never before heard of the Christian faith. Usually it is a presentation to a congregation of Christian people who, whatever their understandings of things Christian, have at least taken the risk of exposing themselves to the gospel. While every sermon should no doubt *announce* the good news to these people, it should also, and for the greater part, be at pains to teach it to them, to help them come to understand it and their lives in relationship to each other.

We ask the question about the central task of ministry because we believe it is one of the matters at the heart of the present crisis in the church. How well ministers understand what is given to and required of them to be and do, and how well they do what is required of them, is both part of the problem faced by churches (particularly the mainline churches) today and part of the solution to this problem. While ministerial self-understanding and its implementation in practice is assuredly not the only factor involved in either the inertia of the mainline churches or overcoming that inertia, nevertheless we can probably say that the problems of these churches will not be overcome *without* a significant transformation in the self-understanding and expectation that ministers have of themselves.

Our claim is that all clergy, regardless of whether they are appointed as parish clergy, as judicatory executives, or whatever, should understand themselves primarily as teachers of the Christian faith. They should be teaching ministers. That should be the focus of their self-identity *as* ministers of the Christian faith; that is what it means to be a minister of word and sacrament. It is that to which ministers are ordained. That is to say, it is not only wrong but decidedly unhelpful and has contributed greatly to the present decline of the mainline churches, when clergy understand themselves in and act in ways fundamentally different from this. If ministers think of themselves *primarily* as administrators of parish activities or *primarily* as psychotherapists, they will probably pay insufficient attention to the one thing for which the church sets aside ministers for itself in the first place. That one thing is to insure that there will be people in the church whose task it is both to make and to interpret the Christian witness, to proclaim and to make sense of the Christian faith.

We do not wish to be misunderstood on this, but it strikes us that if clergy think of themselves as pastoral-directors, in H. Richard Niebuhr's phrase, the emphasis over time shifts to the "director" part of that title. Ministers are then tempted to become experts in manipulating the technology of administration, as though that in itself addressed the existential needs of people. It also strikes us that if clergy think of themselves as pastoral-counselors, the emphasis over time shifts to the "counselor" part of that title. In this case, ministers are tempted to become experts in manipulating the technology of psychotherapy, as though that in itself addressed the existential needs of people.

This is not the place to make the argument that supports this claim. In a way, that is part of the task of this book as a whole. In the first chapter we review much of the sociological and theological literature of the last few decades that describes the plight of mainline churches and contend that all this literature makes direct connections between the crisis of the church today and the function of the ministry. The sociologists know what the church sometimes seems not to know: that theology is important, that the irreplaceable function of the church is to help people understand their lives in the light of ultimate reality and understand ultimate reality in the light of their lives. They know, in the words of an author whom we discuss later, that it is important to think about the question, What does the church have to say that no other group can be relied on to say? We suggest that only a serious revival of ministers' understandings of themselves as *teachers* of the Christian faith will address the problem of the "secularization from within" that is so characteristic of mainline churches today and so much at the heart of their lack of a distinctive Christian identity.

Furthermore, we seek to show that something like this understanding of ministry as involving teaching and interpreting the faith has always characterized the life of faith—in the history and literature of biblical Israel, in the practice and writings of the earliest churches as recorded in the scriptures, and throughout the history of the church until recently. Indeed, the first half of this book is dedicated to showing the urgency of recovering what is in fact a very old self-understanding of ministry and to showing that the church has never been without witnesses to the importance of teaching as an indispensable component of the life of faith itself and therefore of ministry.

The latter half of the book fleshes out the contention of the first half in more concrete and constructive terms. There is a nuts-and-bolts approach to doing theology: that is, to learning how to ask theological questions, an approach that situates theology in the life of the church. Also, there is a chapter suggesting homiletical approaches to sermons that enable them to be teaching occasions and a chapter on other ways in which the minister can and ought to be a teacher in the congregation.

We wrote this book as follows: Ron Allen wrote the chapters on teaching in the tradition of Israel, on the sermon as a teaching event, and on other ways of teaching in the church. Clark Williamson wrote the chapters on membership loss and theological discernment, on teaching in the history of the church, and on teaching and theology. Each chapter was then revised in the light of our responses to each other. We would like to express our thanks to Charles Blaisdell, Brenda Brasher, Bruce Roberts, Arthur Vermillion, Marti Steussy, and Newell Williams for giving us their critical responses to previous versions of these chapters, and to Nelle Slater for suggestions about teaching and for calling to our attention several papers on the teaching office of the church.

We dedicate this book to our students at Christian Theological Seminary, with the prayer that by God's grace they will be faithful teachers of the Word in season and out.

R.J.A.
C.M.W.

1

MEMBERSHIP LOSSES AND THEOLOGICAL DISCERNMENT

This book is about the central role of the pastor as a teacher of the Christian faith. That teaching the faith has always been inseparable from proclaiming it, that *didache* is necessary to *kerygma*, is its central thesis. That recovery of this understanding and its practice is crucial for today's church is the burden of this chapter.

Here we are concerned with the relationship between the decline of the once-mainline churches and the pastor's task of teaching the Christian faith. We do not think that declining numbers are the central question facing the church today. We do think that radical slumps in membership can constitute occasions for the church to reflect on the question of what it is given and called to be and do as the people of God in today's world.

Stating the constructive thesis of this chapter is a bit tricky. First, there are many reasons for membership decline other than the absence of lively teaching of the Christian faith. Mainline baby boomers as adults have not tended to affiliate with churches. Upward-mobility switching, whereby salespeople who have become executives also switch from the Nazarenes to the Presbyterians, has declined. Mainline families are smaller, thus drying up what was once the largest pool of new members. All these factors contribute to mainline decline.

Second, there is no direct correlation between a church's faithfulness to its task and its "success," particularly if success is numerically quantified or measured in worldly terms. A church might decline precisely because it is faithful to the gospel. Or it might be highly "successful" in secular terms by peddling something other than the gospel—a "feel good" religion, "karate for Christ" lessons in the basement, or any number of self-help therapies adequately attuned to the popular devotion to self-fulfillment. Or it might succeed by setting forth a sentimentalized version of the "old-time religion," or whatever it is that passes for such when the "champagne lady" sings "The Old Rugged Cross" while wearing a diaphanous gown.

Third, theologically a church is successful when it is faithful to the gift that defines its calling, no matter what the statistics say. In this sense, decline is not a sign of failure. But it is the logical fallacy of "false conversion" to conclude that decline and loss are indications of faithfulness. They may be, but then again they may not.

In this chapter we focus on one source of membership decline not mentioned above—the growing number of Americans who list their religious affiliation as "none." Those claiming no religious affiliation have grown from 2 percent of the population in the 1950s to 9 percent in the 1980s (McKinney and Roof 1987, 16). The chief competition for members faced by mainline churches does not come from "right-wing" churches, but from the growing conviction among people that one can be a perfectly good Christian without participating in the life of a church. When we look at the disaffiliation rate, the question of what the mainline churches have been doing wrong takes on a new significance. To some extent, our failure to teach the Christian faith in a compelling and lively way has contributed to our decline.

Mainline Churches: Derailed or Hooked?

A significant body of literature has been produced since the late 1960s outlining what is widely regarded as a crisis in the so-called mainline churches. The term "mainline" is borrowed from railroading, where it refers to a principal line as distinct from a branch line. A main line is a through route. Analogies to the church are irresistible. Once comfortable with rolling through American culture and society on the main line, some churches now find themselves "sidelined." Others have been so stymied in growth and vitality that we can speak of them as having been "derailed." The upper-class Mainline neighborhood in Philadelphia was so named because it was on the railroad's main line. It is a fashionable neighborhood with fashionable churches. Like neighborhoods, churches can decline, and the mainline ones have.

The term "mainline" has also been appropriated by the drug culture. A main line is a major, easily accessible vein of the body into which narcotics can be injected, a process known as "mainlining" and a more immediate way of getting "high." Exploiting this metaphor to describe the mainline churches is tempting and, perhaps, revealing. Did these churches get so "hooked" on their identification with mainstream American culture that they forgot their essential task? Did they get high on a fashionable place in American culture and lulled to sleep? In doing so, did they start increasingly to neglect "the one thing necessary" to a vital church? Or is the better railroad metaphor the caboose, simply following the rest of the train, reacting to what has gone before? Fewer freight trains pull cabooses these days; they are regarded as superfluous.

It is our thesis that the mainline churches have *tended* to avoid their most basic and essential task—teaching the Christian faith. Far too often, those ordained to the ministry of word and sacrament forget to ask themselves what it is that is given to and required of the church to say. Seldom does the church ask, What do we have to say that no one else can be counted on to say? Do we recognize that even if some others *might* say it, nonetheless that does not let us off the hook? Nor does the church follow up that question with the next one: How can we say what we are given and required to say in ways that are appropriate to the Christian faith and adequate to the situation to which we must address what we have to say? To wrestle with questions such as these in the context of the church *is* to teach the Christian faith. Yet this is precisely what happens far too seldom in the mainline churches.

The diagnostic thesis of this chapter is not just the idiosyncratic opinion of the authors of this book. We will try to show that it appears amply in the large body of literature that analyzes the plight of the mainline churches in America today. The constructive thesis of the chapter is that this literature and the volumes of theological reflection accompanying it call for the reemergence of teaching in the church. What is called for is not simply Christian education as we have known it, but theological education *in the church*. We emphasize the phrase "in the church," because theological education has been largely segregated within seminaries and divinity schools, lay people having been kept safely immune from it. If churches are to teach the Christian faith, they will have to engage in theological education. Pastors will have to become pastor-teachers who take it as their task to convey the excitement and depth of the Christian faith to their parishioners.

The Diagnostic Thesis: Neglect of Teaching

In 1969, Jeffrey Hadden raised a tempest of controversy with his book *The Gathering Storm in the Churches*. His central thesis was that the mainline Protestant churches were embroiled in a deep crisis that had the potential to "seriously disrupt or alter the very nature of the church." The struggle, he claimed, was "over the very *purpose* and *meaning* of the church" (Hadden, 5). It was "a crisis of *belief*" because the laity had not been engaged in the theological work of reinterpreting the Christian faith for a new situation; consequently, it was also a crisis of authority, specifically that of the clergy (Hadden, 6).

Ministers had lost their authority as authentic teachers of the Christian faith, Hadden maintained, largely because they had not exercised it. They "have developed a new understanding of the meaning and implications of the Christian faith. They have not succeeded in communicating this understanding to the laity" (Hadden, 230). He predicted that this crisis of authority would come to a head over the involvement of clergy in social and political issues. No longer able to proclaim "Thus saith the Lord," the clergy need to provide a convincing theological and ethical rationale for their understanding of the implications of the Christian faith, one that is appropriate to the Christian tradition. By "theological," Hadden means more than biblical: "The world knows all too well that a scriptural text can be used to justify almost anything, including war, racism, and silence while a nation commits genocide" (Hadden, 233).

Once a task for which pastors assumed major responsibility, teaching has now become the domain of others (Hadden, 217). By "teaching," Hadden means the reinterpretation of the Christian faith in ways that are adequate to the contemporary situation in which the church finds itself and defensible in the light of the Christian faith, ways that are arguably Christian. In other words, teaching means *theological* education in the church. Whereas this was once a key component in the task of everyone ordained to the ministry of word and sacrament, it has fallen into neglect. The result has been a crisis of identity for mainline pastors (Hadden, 211).

Around the time Hadden's book appeared, clergy were widely concerned with this identity crisis, but instead of redefining themselves in the tradition of teachers of the Christian faith, they chose, by and large, to regard themselves as "professionals" at ministry, self-consciously borrowing models of identification from law and medicine. This was a mistake. The crisis in the mainline church was largely theological: "There is no consensus as to what is to be believed, as to what is central and what is peripheral, nor is there any clear authority to resolve the uncertainty" (Hadden, 66). What the clergy needed and still need to do is "to explore openly and honestly the crisis of belief" (Hadden, 234). They need to think and teach theologically, not in an authoritarian, dictatorial way, but in persuasive and convincing ways. The church needs its clergy to become pastor-teachers, pastors who teach the Christian faith.

A Dying Church?

Just three years after the publication of Hadden's work, Dean M. Kelley brought out his *Why Conservative Churches Are Growing*, in which he contended that liberal or mainline churches were actually dying, not merely declining or ebbing. He detected in them "a loss of vitality more significant and perhaps more fatal than a temporary lull," which is why he used the drastic term "dying" (Kelley, ix). Kelley's purpose and point, somewhat overlooked in the debate his book aroused, was that religion performs "a unique and indispensable service," a service too often ignored by church leaders. The unparalleled and essential function of any religious group is to help its members "make sense of the earthly predicament" (Kelley, x).

Following two chapters of detailed statistics laying out the decline of the liberal/mainline churches, Kelley turned to his theme of the essential function of religion. Grounding his remarks on the work of sociologists and cultural anthropologists, he argued that the job of religion from time immemorial has been that of *"explaining the meaning of life in ultimate terms"* (Kelley, 37). The human being, Kelley declares, "is an inveterate meaning-monger . . . a *meaning-oriented being"* (Kelley, 38–39). Not as instinctually programmed as the other animals, human beings find it necessary to construct a human world in which they can live. Each religion is an example of such world building. This world is kept going "by the transmission of its humanly constructed and collectively shared meanings from each generation to the next" (Kelley, 41). Regardless of how they are viewed by outsiders, those religious groups are successful which can interpret the meaning of life in ultimate terms in ways that make sense to their members (Kelley, 45).

Paul Tillich's understanding of religion as "ultimate concern" is involved in Kelley's analysis. An object of ultimate concern not only promises ultimate fulfillment, but makes ultimate demands on its adherents. Hence Kelley's analysis focuses on *both* sides of the theological task—articulating the meaning of life in ultimate terms and explicating what that demands or requires of people who so understand themselves. So he also charged the mainline churches with requiring too little: "If it costs nothing to belong to such a community, it can't be worth much" (Kelley, 53).

Yet it was the neglect of meaning, of teaching the meaning of life amid our earthly predicament in ultimate terms, that was at the heart of Kelley's concern with mainline Protestantism. He was convinced that far too often leaders forgot the true business of any genuinely religious organization, which is "communicating the *meaning* of life which the religious group wants to proclaim" (Kelley, 136). Kelley was not opposed to social work or political action. He opposed the failure of the church to teach the Christian faith in such a way that the understanding of what faith requires in the present was linked to reasons why these requirements follow from an understanding of the Christian faith. Probably Kelley could have made his own case more convincing had he shown how taking seriously the theological task of the church would have helped accomplish precisely what he thought necessary. Yet his analysis of the plight of the mainline churches defines the problem in the same way Hadden had already done: the problem is the failure of the church to interpret the Christian faith in a way both appropriate to its claims to disclose ultimate meaning and truth and adequate to the ever-changing world in which we live.

Secularization From Within?

The extremity in which mainline churches find themselves has been analyzed as constituted by what the sociologist Thomas Luckmann called "secularization from within . . . the substitution of secular for religious contents within the mainline Protestant churches" (Berger, 24). Peter Berger contends that too many mainliners forsake the task of bearing witness to the tradition in preaching and through the sacraments in favor of a left-wing ideological agenda (Berger, 34–35). Regardless of whether he is correct in this claim, it is the case that failure to teach the Christian faith in the church creates a vacuum that will be filled by something else, and that something else will be some kind of culture-bound religiosity.

Sociologists William McKinney and Wade Clark Roof unearthed an important piece of data in their 1986 study of mainline churches. The chief competition these churches face for members is not the more conservative churches but "dropping out of religion altogether" (McKinney and Roof 1986, 46). Among liberal Protestants of the older generation, the net loss is 3.1 percent; younger mainliners drop out into religious nothingness at an 8.7 percent rate (McKinney and Roof 1986, 47). It is not denominational switching, but defection altogether that is the problem for mainline churches, and this defection "is becoming common indeed among liberal Protestants" (Hammond, 62).

In 1987, McKinney and Roof shed yet more light on the tendency of mainline Protestants to drop out of religion. Between 1952 and 1985, the percentage of the population expressing a religious preference for Protestantism dropped 15 percent (McKinney and Roof 1987, 16). Since the fifties the greatest increase in religious affiliation has been that recorded under the category "none." In the eighties, 9 percent of the population identify themselves as unaffiliated with any religious tradition, compared to 2 percent who did so in the fifties. Also, in the 1980s at least ten of the biggest Protestant denominations were undergoing a serious religious depression, their membership declines about equaling the percentage of people who have defected from religion altogether (McKinney and Roof 1987, 151).

Although McKinney and Roof do not directly address the issue of teaching the Christian faith, they come close to the heart of the problem. They point out that the mainline churches enjoyed an artificial prosperity in the fifties, that they became "something of a 'culture-religion,' . . . captive to middle-class values, and somewhat lacking in their ability to sustain a strong transcendent vision" (McKinney and Roof 1987, 22). Consequently, the "big losers" among the denominations are the moderate Protestants—Methodists, Lutherans, Disciples, American Baptists, Presbyterians (McKinney and Roof 1987, 171). The chief reason such groups have been unable to hold their own is their "close identification with the mainstream culture" (McKinney and Roof 1987, 172). Their defection rate to the ranks of the unaffiliated is about 8 percent, which represents people who can drift away from church involvement without, apparently, missing it. Middle-class values and mainstream culture are available outside the churches. The failure of church life to offer a vision transcending the culture undercuts any reason for participating in the church.

This analysis is confirmed by the work of Robert Wuthnow in *The Restructuring of American Religion.* While his book looks at the momentous social changes that have taken place in American society since World War II, as well as at the deepening rift between conservatives and liberals, he, too, takes seriously other reasons for the declining levels of religious involvement (Wuthnow, 159). He notes that "a sizable number of the better educated who switch denominations cease to affiliate with *any* denomination" (Wuthnow, 171). Sixteen percent of Methodists and 19 percent of Baptists with college educations who cease being Methodists or Baptists simply defect from religion altogether, listing their present affiliations as "none" (Wuthnow, 171).

What is of concern to mainline Protestant churches about this is that while the populace in general is becoming better educated, the better educated denominations have failed to grow in overall membership

(Wuthnow, 171). These churches fail to attract members from precisely that segment of society to which they should find it easiest to appeal. Like our other analysts, Wuthnow, too, notes the failure of mainliners to take with sufficient seriousness the theological task of the church, the explanation of the meaning of life in ultimate terms (Wuthnow, 294–307).

To some extent, the American emphasis on religious individualism may account for this loss of members to the ranks of the unaffiliated, but when we consider for how long religion has been privatized in America, this explanation is unconvincing. The question we should be asking is, How can people leave mainline churches and, to all intents and purposes, not notice anything important missing from their lives? Has the failure to teach the Christian faith, to develop a gathered community of believers in which faith is shaped and nurtured, meant that these people do not miss what the church has to offer because, too often, the church is not offering it? If what the church has to offer is simply a blessing of the major values and causes of the culture in general, cannot people have direct access to those without the extra bother of church involvement?

Recovery of the Teaching Task

Faced with a radical religious individualism on the one hand and a too-simple conservative/evangelical religious alternative on the other, what are the mainline churches to do? In *Habits of the Heart*, Robert Bellah and his colleagues have this to say about the situation of the mainline churches:

> Without the leavening of a creative intellectual focus, the quasi-therapeutic blandness that has afflicted much of mainline Protestant religion at the parish level for over a century cannot effectively withstand the competition of the more vigorous forms of radical religious individualism, with their claims of dramatic self-realization, or the resurgent religious conservatism that spells out clear, if simple, answers in an increasingly bewildering world (Bellah, et al., 238).

In the last century, mainline/liberal Protestantism has been changed from a church that was "on the move" to one that is "on the defensive" (Gaustad, 99). "Until theology becomes once more an energizing source," declares Edwin Gaustad, "until corporate worship is revived, until transcendence is believably affirmed, the spiritually hungry are unlikely to be fed—at least by us" (Gaustad, 101). Liberal Protestantism may be addressing the wrong problem, that of helping people escape from the authoritarianism of fundamentalist religion. Today its task may be to address instead the unchurched or once churched with the vision of an authentic

Christian faith theologically articulated (Zikmund, 185). A major weakness of the liberal churches is clearly the depletion of their theological resources. One function of theology, argues Benton Johnson, is that it "mobilizes the collective energies of a religious community. When a community's theological resources drain away, its energy level declines" (Johnson, 222). Clearly, the importance of the teaching ministry of the church, understood as theological education in the church, is paramount if mainline churches are to get back on track.

Hence, Timothy L. Smith, in his study of how evangelical (Protestant) Christianity in America both created and circumscribed a pluralistic culture oriented toward ideals of peace and justice, concludes with this address to religious leaders in late twentieth-century America: "Your first duty is to be truly what you are, to drink again from the wells dug by your father Abraham, to let the Holy Scriptures speak their persisting message of *shalom* to your own mind and heart" (Smith, 16–17).

Dean Kelley's use of the drastic term "dying" to describe the situation of the once-mainline churches was probably overdrawn. More recently, membership declines in these churches seem to have leveled off (although decline continues), while growth among conservative churches is no longer as striking as it once was (Hunter, 32–35). Nonetheless, mainline churches face several significant problems other than numerical decline. One is that the leadership of these denominations has failed to bring along their constituencies effectively; there is a great gap between the views of the laity and those of denominational leaders on social, economic, and political issues (all of which are moral issues). There is a significant educational gap between laity and clergy, as well as between denominational and ecumenical leaders and laity. Laity are effectively deprived of theological education, while leaders who have at least been exposed to it wonder why laity do not share their views on a host of complex issues! The prospect of a "storm" in the churches, which Hadden suggested, has not disappeared, nor have those laity who disagree with the more politically liberal stances of their leaders simply picked up and left the mainline churches: "With few exceptions, the mainline laity remains socially and politically quietistic, aloof from the enthusiasms of its leadership" (Hunter, 42).

Too Comfortable or Too Prophetic?

At this point, a potential confusion needs to be clarified. Readers will have noticed that two different, and possibly contradictory, criticisms have been offered of mainline churches. On the one hand, they are charged with "culture religion," that is, waving a wand of benediction over the values of middle-class culture. On the other, they are indicted for taking liberal or radical political stands that go directly counter to the values of their middle-class constituents and of not bringing that constituency along on the issues. Which is the case, if either? "Are mainline churches weak because they attack the culture or because they bless it?" (Derr, 61).

The answer to this question is probably: both, in different respects. That is, at the leadership level (for example, policy statements from General Assemblies, stances of independent boards, positions taken by various commissions and ecumenical bodies), the mainline churches tend to take decidedly liberal views on a wide range of social issues. At the same time, at the level of local congregations, the great likelihood is that little or nothing will ever be said or heard about these very same issues. General assemblies of the church tend to have a life of their own, apart from the goings-on in local congregations. Topics will be voted on and passed in such assemblies, topics that are regarded as "too hot to handle" in local congregations. It should not come as a surprise, therefore, when members of those congregations are shocked to read in the newspaper that their church holds strong positions on a wide range of controversial issues, issues that those laity had never heard discussed in church.

This suggests that different parts of the church fail to interact, that they are more like different levels of one church or almost totally autonomous from each other than they are like intersecting dimensions of one church. It also suggests a dual failure to teach the Christian faith. Locally, there is a lack of teaching that seeks to relate the meaning of the Christian faith to the more troublesome issues of the day, and at the leadership level there is a failure to lay out the grounds and warrants, the arguments, that would lend credence to the claim that various stances taken are either compatible with or required by the Christian faith. If leaders fail to make the connection between a stance on homosexuality or abortion, say, and the Christian faith, how can they be critical of followers for failing to see it?

By now, the argument should be clear enough: a major task facing the mainline churches today is recovery of the teaching ministry, one that is committed to engaging the important issues of the times from a perspective solidly grounded in the Christian faith. This approach to the culture would seek neither to withdraw from it in sectarian fashion, in order to set forth an unalloyed Christianity, nor to dissolve the Christian faith into the culture; it would avoid both the "Christ against culture" and the "Christ of culture" positions and seek instead to be attentive to the one thing necessary—asking and answering the question of what is given to and required of the church to say that no one else can say—and at the same time seeking to engage this one thing, the gospel of Jesus Christ, with the signs of our times. The church needs to rediscover its center.

The Constructive Thesis: Centering
in the Christian Faith

While sociologists and historians have been diagnosing the predicament of the mainline churches, theologians have also attended to the situation in which these churches find themselves. Throughout this period, roughly the last two decades, they have offered a series of proposals to help the derailed mainline churches get back on track.

The Heart of the Matter

Long ago, Martin Marty dealt with the problem faced by what he called the "old dominion denominations," saying: "in Protestantism, the 'old, worn-down' denominations are wearing further down, while the 'young, rugged' denominations are being pushed up higher and are offering an ever more jagged and prominent skyline" (Marty, 82). These older denominations had long taken responsibility for relating religion positively to the culture; they were largely established and became the establishment. Most exposed to the social-cultural environment and least protected by sectarian tendencies, they became "the most secularized by long erosive tendencies" (Marty, 83).

Sagely, Marty counseled his readers not to be misled by the typically American equation of growth and success with faithfulness to the truth. Being enamored with success can work in two diametrically opposite ways: groups that are growing can point to their growth as itself the sign of their truthfulness, while groups that are shrinking can claim their smaller size as a sign of their greater faithfulness to the gospel. After all, did not Jesus call the church a "little flock"? Yet growth may simply mean that the growers are cagey about offering only what they know will sell, and decline may be not so much a sign of greater faithfulness as of general ineptitude.

Marty contends that the mainstream Protestant churches "have themselves to blame for their troubles" (Marty, 120). The mainstream's problem is its "boundarylessness," its tendency to disperse its energies into the surrounding world. The task before the mainstream is that of "centering"

(Marty, 141). But because our people and culture need churches that can communicate, boundarylessness is not *all* bad; it is better than the restrictiveness of the more introverted churches that are out of communication with the pressing issues of the time (Marty, 147). The question Marty raises is, How can churches be open without loss of identity, or how can they be centered without being closed off? He answers both questions with the concept of "coring" (Marty, 219–233).

The core "is the central or universal part, the 'heart' of anything" (Marty, 219–220). "Core" is related to the French word for "heart" (*cœur*), from which "courage" is derived. As Tillich might have put it, the church needs "the courage to be itself." For the church to find its heart is to find the courage to proclaim and teach what is at its heart and what it is given and required to proclaim and teach. A church that knows its heart—the gospel of Jesus Christ, which promises the love of God freely to each and all and requires in turn that we love God and do justice to all those whom God loves—will neither dissipate into the culture at large nor close itself off from its context. Instead, it will have a "magnetic center" (Marty, 220), a heart that attracts, and openness at the edges.

The best way for mainliners to recover the heart of the church is for clergy to take more seriously their central task of teaching the Christian faith. The problem facing the mainline churches is not so much narrowness as it is disintegration, loss of the center. To recapture the heart of the matter, mainliners must take responsibility for the Christian tradition. By "tradition," we mean two things: first, that which in every generation we inherit from the past, that body of Christian wisdom which is given to us and which we do not have to reinvent; second, the act of "passing on" (which is what the verb *traditio* means) what we have received to the next generation. Not knowing our tradition leaves us confused; not passing it on creatively and critically transformed identifies us with the past and leaves us closed off from the present.

Transcendence and Relevance

The question Marty raised was earlier posed by Langdon Gilkey, in different terms: "How," he asked, "can the church minister to the world, which is its task, without losing itself, which is always its danger?" (Gilkey, 1). If the church is to be itself and carry out its charge, it must present to the world "some Word, some Presence, some norm and standard, that are both transcendent in their origin—in some measure 'holy'—and also relevant to the world's life" (Gilkey, 2). But, at present, the church is in danger of losing itself, its authority being diminished, its life in danger of being engulfed by the world, its identity with middle-class society and the free-enterprise system almost complete (Gilkey, 17–35). It is more a mirror in which the world can see itself glorified than a beacon of light shining into the world's darkness.

Aware that "the church can never take itself for granted" (Gilkey, 74), which mainliners have been tempted to do, Gilkey calls attention to the responsibility of ministers as preachers, teachers, and pastors. What they are given and called to do is to pass on *(traditio)* the living word to the congregation, to lead it to "discover God's judgment, mercy, and love which come to us through the apostolic witness in Scripture" (Gilkey, 79). The point and purpose of ordination to the ministry of word and sacrament is to see to it that the public ministry of the word—preaching and teaching—be secured in its place as the church's most important function, on which all else depends. If the word of God's all-inclusive love, graciously offered, and God's all-inclusive justice, radically commanded, is not heard in the church, then the link with Christ "is broken and the church slips back into the world to become nothing more than the world" (Gilkey, 80).

To avoid losing itself, the church must recapture its older tradition that the task of ministers is to speak with authority on matters of the Christian faith, on the understanding of life in ultimate terms. A misunderstanding of the priesthood of all believers leads to the silly conclusion that all members of the congregation are equally educated in the faith and equal in authority when speaking about it. In a church that does not engage in the theological education of its members, this means that the lay voice simply reflects the voice of the culture (Gilkey, 84). First of all, the minister is a servant of the word, charged with teaching and preaching the Christian faith in ways appropriate to it and in the light of which the congregation can understand itself intellectually and morally.

But if congregations are to hear and obey the word, denominations must cease taking alarm at the prospect of thinking theologically and quit opposing the teaching of theology in the church (Gilkey, 85). The church is to be composed not only of those who speak the word, but of those who are capable of hearing it as well. But how can the laity have ears to hear, if they are forever infantilized and never encouraged to learn their tradition and to appropriate it (a constructive move) critically and creatively? Why should the laity be kept unsophisticated in matters of the Christian faith, yet expected to understand highly sophisticated theological and ethical declarations on complex issues, and then blamed for not doing so?

Theology in the Church

As Gilkey calls for a revival of teaching the Christian faith in the church, so Edward Farley argues: "If theology is part of the interpreting life of the believer as such, then its study is a responsibility not just of clergy education but of church education" (Farley 1988, x). Christian theology, as Farley defines it, "is the reflectively procured insight and understanding" that encounter with the Christian faith evokes (Farley 1988, 64). It presupposes that one is coming to terms with the historically given nature of the Christian faith and is an attempt to understand—that is, interpret—that faith. It is the *reflective* or *considered* understanding of the Christian faith, an understanding that is self-critical and keeps checking itself as to its appropriateness to that which it seeks to understand.

Farley wants to know how it is that the Christian faith itself can be committed to relating faith to knowledge, learning, reality, and the world, and yet restrict the attempt to do so to the clergy and deny it to the laity (Farley 1988, 85). Why is it necessary for the clergy to understand scriptures, doctrines, and the moral life, yet not necessary for the laity? Why is the church content to rest in the medieval pattern of an educated clergy and an uneducated laity and to create an "almost uncrossable gulf between theological (clergy) education and church education" (Farley 1988, 85)?

Clearly, these questions are not only pertinent but directly related to the gulf between clergy and laity that almost all contemporary studies of the church make clear. Both the storm in the churches, which Hadden predicted and which is now reflecting itself in a fundamentalist resurgence in several mainline churches, and the defection rate into nonaffiliation show what can happen when laity simply are not given the opportunity to understand the Christian faith in the reflective and considered manner that is required, as a matter of course, for ministers. Yet Farley's questions are so aptly put and so direct, that not to face them is not to face a large part of what is wrong in the mainline churches today.

Recently, I had to discuss with the local congregation of which I am a member the controversial issue of religious pluralism and whether salvation is possible apart from Jesus Christ. The conversation became intense, and the discussion was not what one would call "nuanced." What was disturbing about it, however, was that members of the congregation—judges, lawyers, professors, scientists, engineers, schoolteachers, medical doctors, and business people, all people with considerable ability and capable of carrying out complex tasks—were still at an elementary-school, literalist level in their understanding of the Christian faith. The only resource they had with which to approach the question of whether salvation is possible apart from Jesus Christ was a few scraps of biblical knowledge, however well or poorly understood. It was as if the Christian tradition had not been wrestling with complicated issues for the last two thousand years! The only explanation for how this is possible seems, finally, to be the one offered by Farley: "The church continues on the assumption that ordered learning *with respect to matters of religion*, its texts, history, belief, and practices, is not a possibility for the believer" (Farley 1988, 94).

As one church historian puts it, "the fundamental issue facing the . . . mainstream denominations is not denominational identity; it is Christian identity" (Bass, 10). A recovery of denominational identity would be important as and only as it aided in the recovery of Christian identity. Meanwhile the chief failure of the mainline churches "is an educational failure: a failure to transmit the meaning and excitement of Christianity from one generation to another" (Bass, 11). This failure stems from an inability among mainliners to draw on the tradition as a vital source of faith and life and results in an accommodation to the culture; greater attention to creating opportunities for theological education in congregations is a significant part of the answer to the plight of mainline churches today (Bass, 13).

Clearly, a new approach not only to preaching—preachers must teach as well as proclaim—but to education in the church is required. Farley suggests that "the educator on the church staff will have to be a theologian-teacher" (Farley 1988, 99). That is fine for churches that have a multiperson staff; most do not, having only one pastor. That pastor, educated theologically, must understand her- or himself as a teacher of the Christian faith and set about teaching in a theologically responsible way. Ministers are pastor-teachers who must be good educators. This understanding of ministry as teaching the Christian faith, really a very old understanding, is the greatest need facing all of today's churches, but particularly those once on the main line.

2
TEACHING IN THE TRADITION OF ISRAEL

In Judaism and Christianity, renewal often begins with rediscovery. We come upon roots that have been neglected, or misperceived, and we discover afresh that they have the power to bring forth a fresh sense of God's presence, purpose, and power.

We proposed in the opening chapter that the time is ripe for thinking of ministry as a teaching vocation. In so doing, we are not suggesting something new, but are exposing a root that lies deep in the soil of Judaism and Christianity.

In this chapter we recall the central and generative place of teaching in the formative literature of the Jewish and Christian communities (compare Crenshaw 1985). Three notes of orientation are in order. First, we do not see a systematic distinction in the biblical traditions between preaching and teaching. While we can sometimes see differentiation (as, for example, in the difference between missionary preaching and prebaptismal catechesis), the differences are largely of focus of content for particular audiences rather than of fundamental mutual exclusion. Second, we recognize that the communities who wrote the canonical literature did not have religious leaders who are precise parallels to contemporary ministers. The minister of today is the heir of diverse traditions of leadership ranging from the priest to the early Christian prophet. Yet, while we cannot always point to a one-to-one correlation between ministerial roles in past and present, we think that current clergy can be helped in coming to clarity concerning the teaching work of the pulpit by remembering the pervasiveness of the teaching function in our tradition. Third, we cannot be limited to "word studies" of the key Hebrew and Greek terms for preaching and teaching but must keep an eye on the broader function of preaching and teaching in the canon.

Deuteronomy

The book of Deuteronomy is a good beginning point because its discussion of preaching and teaching is a finely ground lens through which to view much of the development of these motifs in the Hebrew Bible. Deuteronomy is presented as a series of sermons from Moses. The Deuteronomic Moses is "a preacher who uses skillful oratory to move his congregation to consider issues of life and death urgency" (Anderson, 378). These sermons are important to our topic in four ways.

First, they repeatedly underscore the utter centrality of teaching and learning in the whole community of Israel. Indeed, God is the great teacher of Israel (Deut. 4:10). Teaching permeates the responsibility of Moses (for example, 1:5; 4:14; 6:1), the priests (for example, 33:10), the prophets (13:1–5), and the parents (11:19). Even the king is to be a constant learner (17:18). Indeed, God says, "And these words which I command you this day shall be upon your heart; and you shall teach them diligently to your children, and shall talk of them when you sit in your house, and when you walk by the way, and when you lie down, and when you rise" (Deut. 6:6–7). Thus, Gerhard von Rad comments, "Deuteronomy is motivated by a desire to instruct such as we find in no other book of the Old Testament" (von Rad 1966, 267).

Second, the Deuteronomic sermons are themselves acts of teaching (for example, 4:1; 5:1). Robert Polzin has shown that, in Deuteronomy, Moses is principally a declarer and teacher. Through careful literary analysis, Polzin has shown that the Deuteronomist seeks for the reader to regard Deuteronomy as having the same interpretative authority in its time as Moses is pictured as having in his (Polzin, 10).

Third, the subject matter of the teaching sermon is *torah* (for example, 1:5; 4:8, 44; 17:19; 28:58; 29:29; 33:4, 10). The Hebrew word *torah* is sometimes translated as "law," but the popular understanding of "law" (as a rule to regulate behavior) is too narrow and restrictive. *Torah* refers, more expansively, to instruction, guidance, or teaching, and, according to James A. Sanders, "it appears that the oldest and most common meaning is something approximate to what we mean by the word *revelation*" (Sanders 1972, 2; see also Schechter, 116ff.).

According to Deuteronomy, the center of the *torah* is the story of the deliverance from Egypt (for example, Deut. 6:20–25) and the making of the covenant at Horeb (Sinai) (for example, Deut. 4:44ff., esp. 5:1–3). The covenant included stipulations that are variously called statutes, commandments, and ordinances (for example, 5:1–21; 10:12–25:19). The people are to *learn* and *do* these statutes (5:1). The commandments "point out the way by which Israel can become, in practical expression, what it already is in theological affirmation" (Clements, 33). The statutes and ordinances picture in concrete ways how love and justice are to be embodied in the covenantal community.

Fourth, Deuteronomy understands teaching to include two closely related moments: remembering and interpreting. The teacher's first task is to help the people remember the tradition (for example, 4:9ff.; 26:1–11, esp. vs. 5–9; see also Childs, 51–54). Then the teacher is to help the people interpret the tradition. Indeed, the purpose of Moses' preaching in Deuteronomy is "to explain this law (*torah*)" (Deut. 1:5). The Hebrew word *be'er* (to explain) refers explicitly to making clear (Craigie, 92); (for example, 4:32–40; 7:6–11; 10:14–15). And this is precisely what the Deuteronomist is continually about: making clear the significance of the traditions of Israel.

The condition of blessing in the community results from right teaching and learning (which are the sources of right practice), while the condition of curse derives from the reverse (for example, Deut. 11:26–28; see also Deut. 28:1–68). Indeed, teaching (and learning) are a matter of life and death (Deut. 30:15–19). Many psalms partake of the Deuteronomic view of teaching (for example, Pss. 25:4–5; 27:11; 34:11; 86:11; 94:12; 119 passim, esp. v. 104; 143:8–10).

Priests, Prophets, and Sages

Priests, prophets, and sages are all identified with teaching in the Hebrew Bible.

Priests

After the Deuteronomic Moses wrote the *torah*, he gave it to the priests (and to all the elders of Israel) and commanded them to read the *torah* to the whole people every seven years (Deut. 31:9–13). The priests are then told to put the *torah* in its book form beside the ark of the covenant (Deut. 31:24–29) where the *torah* will now take its place with the ark as one of the definitive symbols of the people. And Moses blesses the vocation of the Levites: to teach and to preside at the altar (Deut. 33:10; von Rad 1953, 13–15, 66–67).

The priests appear similarly in the books of Chronicles. For instance, at a low point in Israel's history, the Chronicler laments, "For a long time Israel was without the true God, and without a *teaching priest*, and without law (*torah*)" (2 Chron. 15:3). The renewal sponsored by Jehoshaphat is accompanied by the teaching of the priests among the people (2 Chron. 17:7–9; see also 2 Chron. 30:22; 35:3).

Ezra is also described as a scribe "skilled in the law of Moses" (Ezra 7:6) who had "set his heart to study the law of the LORD, and to do it, and to teach [God's] statutes and ordinances in Israel" (Ezra 7:10).

After a group of the people of Israel had returned from the exile, they gathered before the Water Gate (Neh. 8:1). Ezra stood on a "pulpit" (or tower) and read the law of Moses from "early morning until midday, in the presence of the men and the women and those who could understand" (Neh. 8:3–4). The Levites *"gave the sense, so that the people understood the reading"* (Neh. 8:8) (our emphasis). This example becomes the paradigm of the teaching priest.

Prophets

The motif of teaching appears both directly and indirectly in the works of the classical prophets in the Hebrew Bible. Several of the prophets point directly to the importance of teaching (or the failure of teaching) in the community. And much of the prophetic literature falls generally within the parameter of the understanding of teaching in Israel as helping the community remember and interpret.

James A. Sanders points out that the prophets generally interpret the life of the communities of their day in one of two ways. If the community is discouraged and in need of reconstitution, then the prophet supports the community and shows them why they can be confident of God's love. The prophet applies the constituting aspects of *torah* to the people. If the community is not living up to the covenantal stipulations, for example, by following other gods or by practicing injustice, then the prophet challenges the community to rediscover its responsibility as a people who are loved covenantally by God (Sanders 1984, 52ff.). We might think of the prophet as a kind of ombudsperson who evaluates the quality of the community's life (including its teaching) in the light of *torah*.

The prophet of First Isaiah, for example, complains that the people have not taken the divine instruction to heart (Isa. 1:10–17; 5:24; 30:9) but have only learned it by rote (29:3). The elders, prophets, and priests have led the people astray with false teaching (9:15; 28:7–8). Right teaching and learning will be a part of the age of restoration.

> Come, let us go up to the mountain of the LORD,
>   to the house of the God of Jacob;
>   *that he may teach us his ways*
>   and that we may walk in his paths (Isa. 2:3, emphasis added).

This invitation is for "all the nations."

For Deutero-Isaiah, God is the great teacher of Israel (Isa. 48:17). The people, unfortunately, have not hearkened to God's teaching and, hence, have fallen prey to spoilers and robbers (42:24). But, in the new age, all the children of Israel will be taught aright and they will prosper (54:13). In the meantime, Isaiah describes his own prophetic vocation as a teacher in a moving passage (50:4).

Jeremiah is especially distressed by the condition of teaching in Judah. Prophets, priests, sages, and scribes have refused to be instructed in God's way (for example, Jer. 6:19; 17:23; 32:33; 44:10) and have even taught themselves such evils as deception, lying, and idolatry (9:5, 14; 10:2–8). Nevertheless, God persistently taught the community. In the coming days, Jeremiah says, God will put the divine law within the human heart so that one person will no longer need to teach the neighbor, " 'for they shall all know me, from the least of them to the greatest,' says the LORD" (31:34). Indeed, even the nations (gentiles) can learn the true ways of God (12:16).

When the land was "full of bloody crimes," Ezekiel chided the priests for not teaching (Ezek. 7:23, 26; 22:26). Judah, indeed, has taught its children to devour one another (19:3, 6). Not surprisingly, Ezekiel's vision of restored temple and land includes the renewal of authentic priestly teaching (44:23; see also Hos. 6:4; 11:3; Amos 2:4; Micah 3:11; 4:2–3; Hab. 1:4; 2:18–19; Zeph. 3:4; Zech. 7:2; Mal. 4:4).

Sages

One of the distinctive theological aspects of Israel's multifaceted wisdom is its lack of emphasis upon the "salvation history" of Israel. Instead, the sages who wrote the wisdom literature focus upon wisdom (*hokma*) as the center of human life.

> According to Israel's sages, a fundamental order lay hidden in the universe; this ruling principle applied both to nature and to humans. Discovery of this "rational rule" enabled the wise to secure their existence by acting in harmony with the universal order that sustained the cosmos. Conduct, it follows, either strengthened the existing order, or contributed to the forces of chaos that continually threatened survival itself (Crenshaw 1981, 66).

Thus one of the important underlying theological connections of the wisdom movement is that God's purposes are revealed in the natural world (von Rad 1972, 62).

Stress upon the importance of teaching is one of the constant elements in all the books of wisdom known to us. The royal court relies upon sages.

The home is a setting for parental instruction. The sages established "houses of learning," that is, schools, where the wisdom traditions are to be passed on (Crenshaw 1981, 57).

The purpose of teaching in the book of Proverbs is to awaken youth to wisdom and to deepen the wisdom of the mature (Prov. 1:2–7). The book of Proverbs offers specific wisdom perspectives to be learned and acted upon. And, when personified, wisdom herself becomes a teacher (8:1–36).

The name *Ecclesiastes* is a crude Greek translation of the Hebrew *Qoheleth*, which refers to one who teaches in a school or presides over an assembly (Eccl. 1:1). Hence, the book of Ecclesiastes is patently a work of teaching and it testifies to the importance of teachers as heads of religious assemblies in the wisdom communities.

Correct teaching is a major issue in the book of Job. After describing Job's situation (Job 1:1–2:13), the book presents different analyses (teachings) of Job's plight in the form of dialogue between Job and his visitors. The book is concerned that the interpretation of Job's situation be sensible and true to experience (for example, 4:3; 6:24; 8:10; 12:7–8; 22:22; 27:11; 32:7; 33:33; 34:32; 35:11; 36:10, 22; 37:19).

In the Hellenistic age, wisdom became integrated into the *torah* tradition. Indeed, in some writings Torah and wisdom were identified. Ecclesiasticus, for instance, explains the origin, manifestation, and importance of wisdom (for example, 1:27; 6:18; 16:25; 24:27; 33:17; 44:4), but it does so in the framework of Israel's covenantal story (for example, 44:1–50:24). Much the same is true of the Wisdom of Solomon (for example, 2:12; 6:4, 18; 10:1–12:27, 15:18ff.; 16:16; 18:4, 9). The latter work states flatly, "whoever despises wisdom and instruction is miserable" (Wisd. Sol. 3:11), whereas those who seek instruction are brought near to God (6:19–20).

The Synagogues and the Rabbis

The synagogue is sometimes called "the most important institution in Judaism" (Rabinowitz, 579). By the first century of the common era, synagogues were everywhere (Tcherikover, 303, 354) and were an accepted part of Jewish life. They served a triple role: as places of prayer, as houses of study, as centers of community life. Indeed, the synagogue was crucial in helping Jewish people to answer the question, What is essential to being Jewish amid the pressures of Hellenization?

The first-century synagogue service was probably structured as follows (Moore, 291ff., but compare Roetzel, 66):

> the Shema, "Hear, O Israel . . . "
> prayer
> singing of psalms
> reading from the scriptures
> sermon
> benediction

The sermon was given by someone appointed by the head of the local synagogue and was given from a sitting position. Typically, the sermon was an interpretation of the Pentateuch or the prophets.

The forms and content of synagogue sermons were evidently quite diverse (Worley, 60). However, contemporary scholars of the Hellenistic era have not had great success in isolating specific patterns and themes of Jewish preaching that can definitely be located in the synagogue in the period 300 B.C.E. to 70 C.E. (Georgi, 358). Scholars are generally agreed that *instruction* was likely the central element in such preaching (Worley, 60).

The instructional element was prominent in missionary strategy. Like other religions of the Hellenistic age, Judaism developed a strong missionary posture and enjoyed remarkable success in winning converts (Koester, 356–358). Jewish missionary strategy included the development of apologetic literature, the use of the miraculous, and preaching (Fiorenza, 2–3).

Interestingly, the synagogue itself was a place of missionary activity and the sermon played an important role. Dieter Georgi concludes that exposition of scripture was a prominent part of Jewish preaching of the period (Georgi, 84). In fact, the exposition of scripture was an important means whereby a sense of the power and presence of the divine was mediated to those present (Georgi, 137ff.).

Lawrence Wills has recently identified the "word of exhortation" as one form of preaching in the Hellenistic synagogue. This form may illustrate general concerns of Jewish preaching of the period.

The word of exhortation consists of three formal parts: (1) the indicative part, which utilizes scripture and other authoritative material from the past and present to develop a thesis; (2) the conclusion, which indicates the significance of the thesis for those addressed; (3) the exhortation, which calls upon the addressees to act (or think) on the basis of the indicative and the conclusion (Wills, 293–299). Wills finds this pattern also in Acts 13:14–41, in Hebrews, in *1 Clement*, and in several other early Christian writings (Wills, 278–292; compare Black, 1–18).

Jewish materials that were given their final form later than 70 C.E. (for example, the Talmud, the Midrashim) almost certainly contain examples of homiletical material from earlier generations, such as the tractate in the Babylonian Talmud Shabbath 32a-b (Heinemann, 998). But precise identification of such material is still tentative.

Shaye Cohen succinctly summarizes the importance of such developments. "Perhaps the most radical function of scriptural exegesis was that it allowed Jews to affirm undying loyalty to a text written centuries earlier for a very different society living under very different conditions. They could claim loyalty to the sacred text even as they freed themselves from it by interpreting it" (Cohen, 206). Such interpretation is a major purpose of the focus of Jewish preaching in this syncretistic period.

Many synagogues sponsored weekday schools that taught reading and interpretation of the tradition (Hengel, 78–83; Cohen, 120ff.; see also Moore, 308ff.). Late in the Hellenistic age, one rabbinic saying was, "As long as the voice of Jacob is heard in the synagogues and the schools, the hands of Esau (that is, the Empire) will not prevail" (Pesikta 121a, cited in Marrou, 317).

The scribes also taught in the open air. Scribal discussion over matters of interpretation was common in public life.

The role of the scribes and the Pharisees is important in the development of teaching and preaching in Judaism in the Hellenistic age. By the first century, the scribes (sopherim) were widely recognized as interpreters, teachers, and administrators. They were interested in "retaining, adapting, and interpreting the tradition and faith" of the Jewish people (Worley, 66). The scribes were frequently called upon to preach in the synagogues and were prominently involved in the synagogue school system, organizing classes for children, youth, and even adults. In the beth hakeneset, the "school" for adults, the scribes led discussions on the interpretation of the tradition (Worley, 67). The scribal goal was to educate the whole of the people in the tradition (Hengel, 79).

Martin Hengel notices that the book of Ecclesiasticus, representing many other scribal works, seeks to remind its readers that, even in the syncretic Hellenistic era, Jews could assimilate only so much from gentile Hellenism. There were certain beliefs, values, and practices that were of the essence of being Jewish and that could not be given up (Hengel, 131ff.). These could be known only by careful study. Therefore, Ecclesiasticus ends with an appeal:

> Draw near to me, you who are untaught,
> and lodge in my school (Eccl. 51:23).

The Pharisees are not a separate group from the scribes. Ellis Rivkin even proposes that, by the first century, the scribes and Pharisees had become the same group (Rivkin, 233ff., compare Neusner 1979). At any rate, by the beginning of the common era, the Pharisees were known for their distinctive program of interpretation and as vigorous teachers who sought for the people to internalize and practice the piety of Judaism.

The following are among the distinctive marks of the teaching and program of the Pharisees. (1) They stressed that God revealed in *torah* is a God of love, justice, and mercy. (2) They called for absolute devotion to God, especially through the daily practice of love, mercy, and justice. (3) The Pharisees developed oral torah to teach people how to be loving, merciful, and just. The oral law was "commentary" on the written law, but sometimes it was given with almost no reference to written material. In either case it was considered authoritative. Furthermore, each generation was obliged to generate its own unwritten interpretation of the law in the light of changing circumstances and new awarenesses (Rivkin 1978, 223). (4) The Pharisees believed in the resurrection of the dead. This doctrine was crucial because the raising of the dead is the final and definitive revelation of the justice and love of God.

By this period the title *rabbi* was used to identify a person as a respected teacher among the Jewish people. Later the word began to be reserved for those who had been formally trained as interpreters of the law, especially the heirs of the Pharisees (Lohse, 961–963).

Of course, there were many other teaching groups in first-century Judaism. We could even refer to this time of Jewish life as a battleground of conflicting teachings. The Qumran community was gathered around a "teacher of righteousness," and among the community's most distinctive features were its biblical commentaries. The Sadducees were repeatedly in conflict with the Pharisees, in part, because of their different teaching. For example, the Sadducees did not accept the resurrection of the dead. In Alexandria, Philo fused the Judaism of the Septuagint with the philosophy of Middle Platonism. The apocalyptic movement depended largely upon the literary form of the vision to express its distinctive teaching concerning the two ages.

In the critical years after the destruction of the temple, Judaism again faced agonizing questions. What does it mean to be Jewish now that the temple is gone? Why did this tragedy happen? What can we honestly believe about God and about the divine promises? The Pharisees, with their distinctive approach to the interpretation of the law, rallied Judaism and have carried it to the present day.

The Earliest Churches

Unfortunately, as we have shown elsewhere, modern scholarship does not command the methodology to reconstruct the role and character of teaching in the ministry of the historical Jesus (Williamson and Allen, 31–34; see also Ogden 1982, 55ff.).

Similar reservations apply to our knowledge of the preaching and teaching of the earliest Christian communities. We have neither sources nor methodology to speak with absolute certainty. For instance, while the book of Acts surely contains some ancient Christian tradition, the book of Acts in its present form is so thoroughly shaped by Luke that it is almost impossible to ferret out the earliest strands.

The most influential attempt to reconstruct the situation of the earliest communities is C. H. Dodd's *The Apostolic Preaching and Its Developments.* Dodd argues that the earliest churches drove a sharp wedge between preaching (*kerygma*) and teaching (*didache*). Preaching, for Dodd, is "the public proclamation of Christianity to the non-Christian world," whereas teaching is "in a large majority of cases ethical instruction" (Dodd, 7). Scholars today generally agree that Dodd overstated the case. In the sources known to us, preaching and teaching are much more closely intertwined (Worley, 30–32; Mounce, 4–5; Smart 1960, 84–87).

To be sure, the missionary preaching of the church likely had a greater emphasis upon announcement than the preaching (or other public discourse) to an established congregation. The discourse to the established congregation would have more emphasis on upbuilding. But the differences were likely a matter of degree. This would be consistent with the practices of Jewish and Hellenistic religious movements that were contemporaneous with the church (see examples in Fiorenza, especially 2–3; Rengstorf 1964, 137, 141, 149; Friedrich 1964, 707–717, 721–727; Friedrich 1965, 692–696, 700–703, 714–715).

Paul

Paul views the teaching of the gospel as having a critical place in the Christian community. This can be seen in two ways: in his discussion of the teaching role in the church, and in his use of the letter as an instrument of instruction.

Three times in the Pauline corpus, and once in Ephesians, we find lists of charismatic leaders in the early churches (see chart). Scholars of the social world of early Christianity have noticed that, in the Pauline and Deutero-Pauline communities, these lists do not designate hard and fixed "offices" but can more accurately be described as functions that were exercised in the local churches (Meeks, 135; see also Gager, 69–74).

Romans 12:6–8	1 Cor. 12:28–30	1 Cor. 12:8–10	Eph. 4:11
prophecy	apostles (first)	wisdom	apostles
service	prophets (second)	knowledge	prophets
teaching	teachers (third)	faith	evangelists
exhortation	miracle workers	gifts of healing	shepherds
giving money	healers	working miracles	teachers
giving aid	helpers	prophecy	
doing acts of	administrators	distinguishing	
mercy	speakers in	spirits	
	tongues	interpretation of	
		tongues	

Scholars today generally agree that the teacher was preeminently concerned with passing on the tradition of the church and with interpreting the significance of the tradition for the current congregation (Greeven, 20–25; Boring, 79; Dunn, 237; Aune 1983, 202). This would be a particularly important role in congregations comprised largely of gentiles who had little exposure to the interpretive categories of Judaism but who now found themselves in a community whose central figure was a crucified Jew.

The teachers of the church were thus much like the scribes of the Jewish community in that a primary part of their work was the exposition of scripture. Further, many of the early Christian hermeneutical principles and practices were adapted from current Jewish practice (see Doeve). W. H. C. Frend even refers to the early church as "the Christian synagogue" (Frend, 119).

At the same time, given the syncretistic character of the first-century Mediterranean world, the teachers helped the early Christians in relating the main themes of the Christian tradition to important categories of Hellenistic religious and philosophical thought. Dodd (among others) was likely right when he suggested that the teachers also offered instruction in the appropriate Christian patterns of behavior in the light of the beliefs, values, and practices of Hellenistic culture.

Teachers exercised their function in three important settings in the early Christian communities. First was in the preparation of candidates for baptism (for example, Rom. 6:17). Second was in the service of worship itself (1 Cor. 14:6, 20; see also 14:26 and Dunn, 237–238). Third, if the early churches were patterned after the synagogue, we may suppose that the teachers took a leading role in the Christian counterpart of the adult synagogue school.

Yet the functions attributed here to teachers in the Pauline churches were shared, at least in some degree, by others. For instance, David Hill concludes, "It would be wrong to make a too neat differentiation between the functions of teacher and prophet" (Hill 1977, 123; see also Hill 1979, 127ff.). Of course, the prophet and the teacher were not identical (Boring, 79–80), but Hill is quite justified in calling the prophet's ministry one of "pastoral teaching and instruction" (Hill 1977, 114; Hill 1979, 126; see also Boring, 78–80).

Paul alludes to his own ministry as having a teaching dimension (1 Cor. 4:17) and to the mutual interrelationship of preaching and teaching (for example, Rom. 2:21; see also Bartlett, 64–67). Paul also describes his ministry in terms that were used among first-century Jewish people to refer to teaching. For instance, in 1 Cor. 15:3–4, he begins, "For I *delivered* to you as of first importance what I also *received*." The words "delivered" and "received" were technical terms in the Judaism of Paul's day to speak of the passing of sacred tradition from one generation to another (Conzelmann, 251; see also 1 Cor. 4:6; 11:2, 23–26; Phil. 4:9). Paul's use of conventional Jewish and Greek modes of teaching and rhetoric in his letters is well established (for example, Davies 1955; Worley, 91–102; Furnish; Sanders 1977; Stowers). Paul also draws upon a device familiar among teachers in the Hellenistic age when he urges the readers to imitate his own life (for example, 1 Cor. 10:31–11:1; see also Bartlett, 71–74; D. Williams 1967).

We note, as well, that Paul's letters themselves have a teaching quality. The letters bring earlier Christian tradition to bear upon the situations of the Pauline congregations. Frequently Paul gives exposition of the sacred scriptures of Judaism for the upbuilding of his communities (for example, Rom. 4; Gal. 3). The apostle helps the congregations wrestle with current difficulties in the light of the gospel (for example, 1 Cor. 5; 6; 7; 8). Paul illustrates the appropriate Christian use of the religious traditions of Hellenism as, for example, when he takes up catalogs of virtues and vices and puts them in the service of the gospel (Gal. 5:16–24). Paul helps the gentiles interpret their own experience in the light of fundamental convictions and categories of Judaism and Christianity (for example, Gal. 3:1–5). Ironically, most of the letters were prompted by the fact of misleading teaching in the churches (for example, 1 Cor. 2:13; 4:15; 6:12; 8:1; 8:4; 10:23; Gal. 1:10; 3:1; Phil. 1:15–17; 3:2).

The Gospels

The Gospels are not simple biographies but are theological interpretations in narrative form. The figure of Jesus whom we see in the stories of the Gospels is more the literary embodiment of the churches' experience of the risen Lord than the plain recollection of the Galilean Jew.

While each Gospel casts its own light on Jesus, all four Gospels present Jesus in the role of teacher-preacher. He speaks after the manner of the scribes in the synagogues (for example, Mark 1:39; Matt. 4:23; Luke 4:14–15; John 6:59) and in the open air (for example, Mark 4:1; 6:34; 12:35; 13:3; Matt. 5:2; 13:2; Luke 5:3; 8:4; John 6:25; 7:14). A group of disciples gathers around him and he teaches them in much the same way as Jewish and Greek teachers (for example, Mark 3:7–19; 4:34; Matt. 5:1; 10:1–11:1; Luke 5:30; 6:13; John 2:2; 13:12). Jesus expounds scripture and other sacred tradition and interprets its significance for those present, often using methods of scriptural exposition that were familiar among the scribes (for example, Mark 7:1–20; Matt. 5:21–48; Luke 4:16–30; John 7:38–39). He converses with other acknowledged teachers of Israel over the meaning of the traditions of Israel in much the same way that the teachers in Judaism habitually discussed and debated (for example, Mark 12:28–34; Matt. 22:23–46; Luke 10:25–37; 20:1–8). He is repeatedly addressed in these materials by titles typically used to address teachers: Rabbi (for example, Mark 9:5; Matt. 26:25; John 1:38), Teacher (*didaskalos*) (for example, Mark 4:38; Matt. 8:19; Luke 9:38; John 3:2), Master (*epistatas*) (Luke 5:5).

Before we plunge into the worlds of the Gospels, we recall that much of the teaching in the Gospels has an anti-Jewish bias (Williamson and Allen, 39–52). We need to recognize this bias and be careful not to let it warp our hermeneutical use of the Gospels in preaching and teaching (Williamson and Allen, 1–9, 56–72).

Mark

The Gospel of Mark was probably written about 70 C.E. in the aftermath of the fall of the temple. This was a time of intense questioning and uncertainty among both Jews and Christians as well as a time of increasing separation and hostility between the two communities. Mark addressed the various tensions of his community by creating a narrative that appears to be set in the life of Jesus but which uses that setting as a vehicle to speak to Mark's own time.

According to Mark, the fundamental problem of the world is that it is under the rule of Satan and the demons. Through Jesus and the church, God has begun to invade the world, to free it from possession and to manifest God's rule (1:14–15; 3:20–27).

From the beginning, Mark highlights Jesus' role as preacher and teacher. Indeed, Jesus' first act of ministry is a word of preaching that sets forth the main theme of Markan theology (1:14–15). After Jesus calls the first disciples (1:16–20), Mark presents a crucial scene in the synagogue at Capernaum (1:21–28). Jesus teaches with authority (*exousia*). This teaching is so powerful that it frightens the demons who possess a person who is present. Jesus exorcises the demon. The use of the word "authority" to describe Jesus' teaching is important because elsewhere Mark uses it to describe the power by which Jesus and the disciples cast out demons (for example, 3:15; 6:7). The crowd responds to the event by saying, "What is this? *A new teaching!* With authority he commands even the unclean spirits." This posits a twofold relationship between teaching and exorcism: teaching the rule of God is itself powerful enough to cast out demons; exorcisms are themselves acts of teaching.

Mark consistently evokes the teaching theme to summarize Jesus' ministry (2:13; 6:6, 34; 10:1; 12:35), and the teaching theme is prominent at key moments (4:1–2; 6:2; especially 8:31–9:1; 9:31; 11:17–18; 12:35). The apostles are commissioned and act as preachers and teachers (3:14; 6:30).

Mark 13 is an important window into the Markan teaching purpose. That chapter reveals that, for Mark, the world is a personal, social, political, and cosmic chaos (13:5–13). False teaching within the church (5–6, 21–22) is making Christians confused, anxious, and in danger of faltering in faith and witness (11–13). Verse 14 contains an aside that shows that Mark understands the discourse in chapter 13 (and, by extension, the whole of the Gospel) to be for the instruction of the community. "But when you see the desolating sacrilege set up where it ought not to be (*let the reader understand*) . . . " (emphasis added).

Scholars have long noted that the relationship between Jesus (the teacher) and the disciples plays an important role in the narrative. Vernon K. Robbins sees that relationship (like many teacher-disciple relationships in the Mediterranean world) unfolding in three phases. (1) Jesus calls and initiates the twelve (1:1–3:6; Robbins, 75–124). The reader identifies positively with the twelve disciples. (2) Jesus instructs the disciples in the content of discipleship (3:7–12:44; Robbins, 125–170). The reader is also thereby instructed. (3) Jesus bids farewell to the disciples and is separated from them. At the end they flee from Jesus (13:1–15:47; Robbins, 171–

196). The disciples do not know the outcome of the story line, namely that Jesus is resurrected (16:1–8). The reader is thereby left with the question, Will I, now knowing the faithfulness of God as revealed through the resurrection of Jesus, be a faithful follower of Jesus?

David Rhoads and Donald Michie clarify how the Gospel helps the reader answer this question.

> The reader would be reassured by this story in which Jesus predicts all that has happened up to the reader's time—famines, wars, persecutions, the horrible desecration and destruction of the temple, and the appearance of many false prophets and anointed ones. Because these predictions had already been fulfilled in the real world, the reader would tend to trust Jesus when he says that the final establishment of God's rule and the return of Jesus were to occur, not at the time of the war or the desecration of the temple, but very soon after. The narrative also points the follower's hopes for Jesus' return away from Jerusalem toward Galilee and the gentile nations. (Rhoads and Michie, 141).

Thus, the Gospel narrative itself serves to teach the Markan community.

Matthew

Because of its focus on instruction, the Gospel of Matthew has been called a "handbook issued by a school" (Stendahl, 20) or a "manual for teachers" (Grassi, 86; see also L. Johnson 1986, 176). We can see the importance of teaching to Matthew in five ways.

First, teaching is a purpose of the church. At the climax of the narrative, on the final mountain of revelation, the risen Jesus states the purpose of the Matthean church. "Go therefore and *make disciples* of all nations, *baptizing* them in the name of the Father and of the Son and of the Holy Spirit, *teaching* them to observe all that I have commanded you; and lo, I am with you always, to the close of the age" (Matt. 28:19–20, emphasis added). The phrase "all that I have commanded you" refers to the story contained in the Gospel of Matthew. The closing theme ("I am with you always") (see Ex. 3:12, 14; Isa. 43:1ff.) stresses the continued presence of the risen Lord within the community. In his risen presence, Jesus could continue to instruct the community, especially through early Christian prophets (Boring, 43).

Second, teaching is a prominent part of Matthew's portrait of Jesus. Matthew summarizes Jesus' ministry as preaching, teaching, and healing (4:23; 7:29). Indeed, Matthew brings together several great teaching discourses that have obvious didactic purpose (5:1–7:29; 10:1–42; 13:1–52; 18:1–35; 23:1–39; 24:1–25, 46; see also Kingsbury 1986, 45–48).

Third, Matthew makes sophisticated and technical use of first-century scribal hermeneutical principles. O. Lamar Cope even refers to Matthew as a "scribe trained for the kingdom of heaven" (Cope, 10). For example, the antithetical way of speaking found in 5:21–48 ("You have heard it said . . . but I say to you") is well known as a form of teaching and debate among the scribes. Much of the theological content of the antitheses (as of the Sermon on the Mount and, indeed, the Gospel as a whole) is similar to the thinking of Jewish teachers of the period (for example, Lapide, passim; Sigal, 83–118; see further Cope).

Fourth, Matthew has reshaped much of the material he received from Mark and Q to give it an obvious, didactic purpose by paring down the details of events and by accentuating the words and actions of Jesus. This is a clear pattern in Matthew's revision of the miracle stories (Held, 165ff.). For instance, compare Matthew 9:1–8 with Mark 2:1–12.

Fifth, Matthew uses the twelve in the Gospel narrative as successors to the ministry of Jesus and hence as literary figures through whom to speak to the Matthean church. The church is to continue preaching, teaching, healing, and otherwise to carry on in accordance with Jesus' instruction (for example, 8:23; 9:35–11:l; 14:28–31; 16:13–20; 17:24–27; 28:16–20). Indeed, a primary work of the Matthean community is to take Jesus' yoke (that is, Jesus' *torah* as revealed in the Gospel and through the Christian prophets) upon itself and to *learn* from him (11:29; see also 9:13; 24:32).

Joseph Grassi rightly points out that Matthew expects teaching to have two outcomes. One is for the Christian to understand properly the relationship of Jesus, God, and the world. The other is for the Christian to *do* in everyday life what is taught, especially to practice justice and mercy and otherwise to embody the rule of God (Grassi, 91–92).

Luke

Luke-Acts is a literary and theological unity whose instructional character is clear in the preface (Luke 1:4). Several major Lukan scholars think that a significant aim of Luke-Acts was to establish a pattern of teaching, authority, and interpretation that begins with Jesus and stretches from the twelve through the early church through the Lukan Paul to Luke's community (for different perspectives, see Talbert 1970, 201; Talbert 1982, 3–4; Aune 1987, 136–141; Minear, 122ff.; Fitzmyer 1981, 8–11).

We can clearly see the centrality of teaching in Luke 4:16–30. "As his custom was," Jesus enters the synagogue on the Sabbath and is accorded the honor (often given to visiting scholars) of reading the Bible and giving the sermon, which interpreted the biblical text for the upbuilding of the congregation. The Lukan Jesus reads from the Septuagintal text of Isaiah (4:18–19). Jesus correlates the text and the Lukan moment in a statement that interprets both: the age of salvation has begun in the ministry of Jesus (4:20). Luke then has Jesus cite a practical consequence of this theological statement by pointing to the movement of God to gentiles (4:24–27).

Scholars correctly call this event a paradigm for understanding the story of Jesus and the early church in Luke-Acts. It is paradigmatic in two ways. (1) It functions as a theological lens for the Lukan corpus. (2) It illustrates an important work of the Lukan teacher: mutually correlating important texts and traditions, including the Septuagint, Jewish practices and beliefs, the stories of Jesus, and the early church, with the life of the community that is contemporaneous with the interpreter in the light of the community's fundamental conviction (revealed in 4:20). Luke calls attention to the role of teaching in helping people understand the coming of salvation and its consequences (for example, 4:32; 5:5, 17; 6:6; 10:39; 11:1, 28; 12:12; 13:10, 22, 26; 20:1; 21:27; 23:5). The Gospel narrative itself is also a mode of teaching the reader (for example, 1:14–17; 3:4–6; 4:1–13; 5:12–16; 6:20–49; 7:11–17; 9:28–36; 10:25–37; 13:10–17; 16:19–31; 17:11–19; 18:9–14).

In the book of Acts, Luke underlines the importance of teaching in four ways. First, Luke singles out teaching as one of the characteristic elements of the life of the ideal Jerusalem community (Acts 2:42).

Second, Luke repeatedly mentions teaching as a part of the ministry of the early church. Frequently the teaching of the early witnesses brings them into conflict with local authorities (for example, Acts 4:2; 5:21, 42; 11:26; 13:1; 15:35; 17:19; 18:11; 20:20; 28:31). The apostolic council is necessary to deal with inhospitable teaching (15:1; see also L. Johnson 1983).

Third, Luke tells stories that obviously have a teaching effect upon the reader (for example, Acts 2:1–42; 5:1–11; 8:26–40; 10:1–11:18; 17:22–31).

Fourth, Luke puts key statements about teaching into the mouths of characters. The most important of these is Acts 20:17–35. The Lukan Paul charges the elders from Ephesus with their responsibility.

> I know that after my departure fierce wolves [i.e., false teachers] will come in among you, not sparing the flock; and from among your own selves will arise men speaking perverse things [i.e., more false teachers], to draw away the disciples after them. Therefore be alert, remembering that for three years I did not cease night or day to admonish every one with tears. And now I commend you to God and to the word of his grace [i.e., teaching], which is able to build you up (Acts 20:29–32).

The primary work of the overseer is to care for the flock by teaching the word of grace. In so doing, the leader is following the prototype of Paul (Acts 20:20ff.).

John

The Gospel of John was written for a community that appears to have been formally—and bitterly—separated from the synagogue. Perhaps the church had been excommunicated and barred from the synagogue (see John 9:1–41, esp. vs. 22, 34; Martyn). The fourth Gospel was at least partially written to provide important theological guidance for the community in this situation in which it needed authoritative teaching to interpret its life.

Jesus is identified as a teacher early in the Gospel (1:38). Immediately, then, the reader is alerted to expect to be taught (see 3:2; 11:28; 13:13–14). The Gospel narrative itself thus becomes a mode of teaching (Craddock 1982, 3–7).

The Johannine Jesus has come from heaven to reveal God. Jesus teaches (reveals) only what God has taught him (for example, 8:28). Thereby, Jesus makes it possible for those who believe in him to be saved and to enter into the quality of existence known as "eternal life" (for example, 1:9–13; 3:16–21). In the process of revealing God, Jesus also exposes the world as a place of darkness, sin, and death and shows the Jews to be children of the devil (8:12–58) and, therefore, to be unfit teachers.

Jesus' teaching ministry takes place in three ways: (1) revelatory conversations (for example, 3:1–22; 4:1–42); (2) revelatory events (for example, 1:19–34; 2:1–11; 4:46–54; 5:1–9; 6:1–14, 16–21; 9:1–12; 11:1–57; 13:1–20; 18:1–19:42; 20:1–29); (3) revelatory discourses that sometimes interpret a primary Jewish symbol (for example, 5:1–47; 8:12–59; 13:1–17:26).

According to John, teaching continues in the church after Jesus' death. "These things I have spoken to you, while I am still with you. But the Counselor, the Holy Spirit, whom the Father will send in my name, *he will teach you all things, and bring to your remembrance* all that I have said to you" (14:25–26, emphasis added). Thus one essential aspect of the teaching ministry of the Spirit is to cause the community to remember and understand what Jesus said (see Brown 1970, 650–651). Another essential work of the Holy Spirit is to draw out the implications of the event of revelation for the future community. "I [Jesus] have yet many things to say to you, but you cannot bear them now. When the Spirit of truth comes, he will guide you into all the truth" (16:12–13).

This may well be a Johannine way of speaking of the activity of Christian prophets in the Johannine community (Hill 1979, 149–151). And it may be a way of authorizing the teaching ministry of the community as spirit inspired. Peder Borgen hypothesizes that, in John 6:25–58, John takes up the style of a synagogue sermon in order to give the exposition of the meaning of the bread of life (Borgen, 28–51, but see Donfried, 19–48). The presence of a synagogue sermon pattern may suggest that John understands synagogue preaching as an ongoing way whereby the Holy Spirit teaches the community.

In John 21:15–19, Peter (and with him the leaders of the Johannine community; see Brown 1970, 1112–1117) is commissioned to feed Jesus' sheep. In the light of John 10, the reader will know that the feeding of the sheep is a figure of speech that refers to the comprehensive care of the followers of Jesus by making known the revelation of God, that is, by teaching. And the careful reader of Jewish tradition will remember that one of the hallmarks that distinguishes the true from the false shepherd is the quality of the shepherd's teaching (compare Jer. 23:13–22).

The three letters of John seem to presuppose confusion, conflict, and division within the Johannine community. The letters explicitly warn the community against false teachers (for example, 1 John 2:18–25; 4:1–6; 2 John 7). Raymond Brown sees the fundamental conflict to be between two groups, each of which claims to be the rightful interpreter of the Johannine tradition (Brown 1979, 103–144; see also Brown 1984). The author is an elder, who may write as part of a "Johannine school" to identify those aspects of Christian belief and life that can allow the community to "test the spirits to see whether they are of God" (1 John 4:1; Brown 1979, 99–103).

The Pastoral Letters

By the time of the pastoral letters (1 and 2 Timothy and Titus), the churches were developing formal structures of leadership. For instance, the office of elder (sometimes called bishop) had become a central office to oversee the life of the church. While the elders were responsible for many aspects of the congregation's life, the office of elder was the congregation's pivotal *teaching* office (for example, 1 Tim. 3:2; 5:17; Titus 1:9; see also Bornkamm, 667; Beyer, 617). Others could teach, of course, but the elders supervised and "guaranteed" all teaching in the church. The church was fully committed to an established, resident teaching ministry. This trend continued as the church aged (von Campenhausen, 84ff.).

Concern for teaching so permeates the pastoral letters that we are surprised only at the few pericopae in which teaching does not directly appear. The teaching dimension of these letters is particularly urgent because the churches were contending with sophisticated "false teaching," which was claiming the attention and commitment of community members (for example, 1 Tim. 1:3–7; 4:1–10; 6:2b–10, 20–21; 2 Tim. 1:15; 2:23–26; 3:1–9; 4:1–5, 14–18; Titus 1:10–16). The antidote for such heterodoxy is the vigorous teaching of sound doctrine.

The Pastor presents "Paul" as a model for teaching ministry in 2 Timothy. The apostle, in fact, is principally preacher, apostle, and teacher (2 Tim. 1:11) and he has given Timothy a "pattern of the sound words" (1:18) that can keep the congregation until the great day (1:12). This gospel is to be entrusted to others of the faithful "who will be able to teach others also" (2:2; see also 2:3–13).

The "ideal teacher" is described in 2 Timothy 2:14–4:5. The teacher should avoid degenerate habits of talking, thinking, and living (2:14–3:9). Instead, the Pastor charges Timothy to "preach the word, be urgent in season and out of season, convince, rebuke and exhort, be unfailing in patience and in teaching" (4:2). The Pastor calls attention to four resources that will help Timothy with sound teaching: (1) the education in faith received from his mother and grandmother (1:5; 3:14); (2) the sound teaching received from "Paul" (1:13); (3) the example of "Paul's" ministry (3:10–11); (4) the scriptures, probably the Hebrew Bible (Dibelius, 119–120), because they point him to salvation (3:15–17; see L. Johnson 1986, 325–326).

Titus relates teaching to the heart of the work of the elders. The elder "must hold firm to the sure word as taught, so that he may be able to give instruction in sound doctrine and also to confute those who contradict it" (Titus 1:9). Virtually all the assignments of the elders that the Pastor then mentions are carried out through teaching (1:9–3:8).

In 1 Timothy, too, the Pastor sets Timothy's ministry in the framework of teaching (1 Tim. 1:3–7; 4:6, 11; 5:7; 6:26). Much of the letter is explicitly didactic and intended to instruct the reader in specific matters (note 1 Tim. 3:14). The syncretistic spirit of the Hellenistic age is in evidence as the Pastor prescribes positions drawn from Christian tradition (such as 1:12–17, especially 15), Jewish tradition, and Hellenistic religious and philosophical connections. Thus, for the Pastor, the sources and subjects of Christian teaching are as diverse as life itself. The norm by which to evaluate all teaching is its agreement with "the sound words of our Lord Jesus Christ and the teaching which accords with godliness" (6:3).

Conclusion

There are other direct and indirect references to preaching and teaching in the literature of the early church (for example, Heb. 5:12; 6:2; 12:3–11; 13:9; James 3:1–18; Rev. 2:14–15, 24). But they add little to the basic point that teaching is an essential part of the leadership of the Jewish and Christian communities.

The specific content of teaching varies from moment to moment in the Bible. But we may generally say that in almost every time, place, and text, the teacher is one who interprets the present life of the community in the light of its sacred traditions and its experience—and the reverse is true. Experience and reflection sometimes cause the teacher to encourage the community to view afresh its relationship to, and understanding of, the sacred traditions.

3
TEACHING
IN THE
CHURCH

In our first chapter, we sought to show that of all the challenges facing mainstream Protestant churches today, none is as critical as that of teaching the Christian faith. What was traditionally called the "teaching office" of the church has recently become problematical. No doubt there are those who claim that, in fact, the crisis lies elsewhere, perhaps in the failure of the church to evangelize, in the deterioration of preaching, or in the lack of caring congregations. Important as these are, the real emergency of the church is faced only when we take seriously the lack of adequate teaching of the faith in the church. Lively teaching of the Christian faith will reinforce preaching, evangelism, and the creation of caring congregations. Indeed, the very definition of a caring congregation entails teaching the Christian faith in ways that are appropriate to that faith itself and that, in turn, help people to make moral and intellectual sense out of their lives.

A subtheme of our first chapter was the decline of the authority of the minister; commentator after commentator remarked upon the ministry's loss of any clear self-identification as to the role and function of the clergy in the contemporary church. The American theologian H. Richard Niebuhr, in his 1956 study *The Purpose of the Church and Its Ministry*, referred to the ministry as the "perplexed profession" (Niebuhr, 48) and noted that neither ministers nor seminaries "are guided today by a clear-cut, generally accepted conception of the office of the ministry" (Niebuhr, 50). Daniel Jenkins wrote his 1947 work *The Gift of Ministry* to counter what he perceived to be the recent "disintegration of the ministry" (Jenkins, 11). Not only has the ministry "moved away from Christian presuppositions" in its self-understanding, it "has rarely been taken seriously as itself in modern Protestantism and . . . ministers have rarely been regarded for their distinctively ministerial qualities" (Jenkins, 11).

1. Robert S. Michaelsen points out that in the past century in America a number of "types" of Protestant ministers have emerged. He articulates these as follows. "The ministry of cultural Protestantism" is a "culture-accommodating ministry" (Michaelsen, 253). This ministry and the churches that support it "became too closely identified with the causes of the moment," although it also ministered courageously to human needs at times of great national danger. For example, clergy on both sides of the Civil War, North and South, in the words of one of them, "wrote, printed, stumped, talked, prayed and voted in favor of [the] government and fought on the same side" (cited in Michaelsen, 253). The culture-accommodating ministry has "plagued Protestantism in America periodically over the last one hundred—and more—years" (Michaelsen, 254), with large segments of the clergy regularly pledging themselves without reservation to the cause of the moment.

2. The "evangelical minister," typified by Dwight Moody, managed to adapt the techniques of revivalism to the urban scene, "but made little attempt to speak directly to the problems created by burgeoning urbanism and industrialism or to examine their causes critically" (Michaelsen, 255). The evangelical minister's sole concern was the saving of individual souls, one by one.

3. The "liberal minister" reacted to biblical criticism, evolutionary theory, and the variety of social and economic crises in cities in such a way as to align Christian faith with the new movements of free thinking and the social gospel: "Openness to new discoveries of truth and willingness to adjust one's beliefs and practices to them—this became the standard of the liberal minister" (Michaelsen, 258).

4. The "fundamentalist minister" arose in the late nineteenth century in a negative reaction against biblical criticism, evolutionary theory, and the social gospel. Fundamentalists were concerned with closing off the church from "alien" influences and preserving it from change. Fundamentalism's characteristic features include biblical literalism, moralism, individualism, insistence on belief in such "fundamentals" as the virgin birth, and resistance to any scientific theories that, to fundamentalists, contradict biblical literalism.

5. Finally, the minister as "social reformer" sought to apply the gospel in a new way to the socioeconomic needs of the time. Social-gospel ministers studied sociology and economics and, as a rule, felt that theology could safely be set to one side as an unnecessary impingement on the time of the minister or ministerial student.

Ronald Osborn, in a paper on the "Many Faces of Ministry," (cited in

Hough and Cobb, 5–16) sums up this development in a different way when he comments on the ministerial "characters" that have recently traipsed across the ecclesiastical stage: (1) The "Master," the authoritative teacher of Puritanism, will be considered later in this chapter. (2) For both the "Revivalist" and (3) the "Pulpiteer," "oratory replaced instruction as the dominant mode of clergy activity"; whereas revivalists worked as evangelists for the conversion of sinners, pulpiteers worked in settled congregations as stable versions of revivalist oratory. (4) By the turn of the century the "Builder" began to loom large on the scene. The "builders" are those ministers whose learning consisted in the mastery of the techniques that would enable them to increase their leadership effectiveness. Builders are "professionals" at ministry. (5) The "Manager and Therapist" is the most recent and probably today most popular model of ministry among mainline Protestants. Managers are professionals who know the theory of how organizations work; they have control of the technology of organizations; therapists know how individuals work; they have control of the technology of counseling. "What the Manager does for the organization, the Therapist . . . does for the individual" (Hough and Cobb, 16). Ministers who manage well and counsel effectively are today in considerable demand.

We have all known all these different "types" of clergy, sometimes several rolled up in one person. What this variety of types leaves us with, however, is a "portrait of confusion" (Hough and Cobb, 16). What is the purpose of the ministry? What is the point of this job? Our purpose in this chapter is to turn again to the history of the church and ask what light it might shed on this question. We argue here for the constancy throughout the history of the church of the emphasis on the ministry as a ministry of teaching. Ministry is never reducible to one function, be it proclamation, teaching, meeting the needs of the poor, working for justice, or evangelizing. Yet none of these functions of ministry can ever adequately be done apart from teaching the meaning of the Christian faith, and teaching the meaning of the Christian faith may be the one key to understanding all the ministerial functions. If the pastor is a "mediator," in what sense is that so? Perhaps the pastor mediates tradition and self-understanding to a contemporary generation of Christians. If the pastor is to be concerned for the psychological well-being of parishioners, perhaps she or he should exercise that concern by helping those parishioners avoid the intellectual and moral confusion that is at the root of so much emotional disorder. If work for justice is to be done, perhaps the pastor's greatest contribution would be explaining to a congregation why this is so and making for them some connections between the current crisis, whatever it is, and the central teachings of the Christian faith.

In this chapter, then, we turn to the history of the church, looking to what it has to tell us about the teaching office of the church. Before we do that, however, let us say a word about the term "office." As used here, it has two meanings, "task" and "appointment." That is, the teaching office of the church is one way of talking about the church's task of teaching the Christian faith. That this task must be carried out is noted in the other meaning, "appointment." *Someone* must be appointed to do it, so that it will not be left to accident. So the teaching office of the church is one of the main jobs of the church, and the church usually gets that job done by seeing to it that people are appointed to do it. Who are those people? What have they done?

Teaching in the Early Church

Irenaeus (c. 130–c. 200), bishop of Lyons in France from 178 until his death, opposed Gnosticism and docetic christologies (christologies that said Jesus was not a human being but only "seemed" to be so; the Greek word for "seem" is *dokeo*, from which the term "docetism" came) by stressing the traditional elements in the church. He appealed to the "tradition which has come down from the apostles and is guarded by the successions of elders in the churches" (Irenaeus, 129). His work is usually cited in support of the doctrine of apostolic succession, but his real claim was that there was a tradition of authoritative teaching of the Christian faith that had been passed down by a line of teachers who had publicly taught the apostolic faith.

In the ancient church it was the bishop who stood for the fullness of the ministry of the church. In this era, we do not yet have the development of hierarchical bishops. It is best to think of a bishop as a local pastor in solidarity with the people of God in a particular place. In the citation from Irenaeus above, he refers to bishops as "elders." The bishop celebrated at the liturgical assembly, functioned as a prophet, and taught the Christian faith. It was only with the passage of time that presbyters or elders (the terms are synonymous) became, in effect, priests of outlying congregations and responsible to the bishop of a metropolitan area. Irenaeus provides his readers with a childhood recollection of hearing Polycarp teach:

> I can tell the very place where the blessed Polycarp used to sit as he discoursed, his goings out and his comings in, the character of his life, . . . how he would tell of his conversations with John and with the others who had

seen the Lord, how he would relate their words from memory (cited in Williams 1956a, 31).

Another famous Christian teacher from the early centuries is Justin Martyr (c. 100–c. 165), a convert to Christianity from paganism who opened a Christian school in Rome. He refused to worship the emperor and was beheaded. His writings give us the best evidence from around and just after the middle of the second century for the nature of the ministry of the church at that time. In them we see at work the teacher, the lecturer (or reader), the bishop, and the deacon. He describes a Sunday morning worship service in a Roman church as beginning with the reading of the works of the apostles "as long as time permits," moving to a discourse from the bishop, which is followed by prayer and the Eucharist. Then a collection is taken for the needs of orphans, widows, and those in prison. As a teacher, Justin regarded himself as standing in the line of the prophets of Israel, as well as in the apostolic tradition in a "succession" of teachers. As the rabbis did, Justin laid hands on the heads of his disciples after they had finished their course of study with him.

Some time after Justin Martyr, the church found that it could no longer rely on autonomous teachers, some of whom themselves fell into heresy. At this time bishops had to take responsibility for being the chief teachers of the Christian faith (Henderson, 16). Thus bishops became "doctors" (teachers) of the church and, as we have seen in the case of Irenaeus, the claim was made that certain bishops in particular, notably those of Rome, stood in a tradition of authentic teaching and teachers that went back to the days of the apostles. So concerned was Irenaeus with countering the false teachings of the Gnostics that he strongly emphasized the teaching function of the bishop and almost overlooked and certainly downplayed other ministerial functions of the bishop.

In Alexandria, Egypt, Clement (c. 150–c. 215) was responsible for the famous catechetical school. "Catechesis" was instruction given to candidates preparing for baptism into the church. Clement is renowned for his role as a teacher of the Christian faith in the early church; his school was attended by adults because instruction was important when adult converts came into the church from the various philosophies and religions of the ancient world. The early church could not assume that candidates for baptism already understood the Christian faith. Clement viewed a true presbyter (teacher) of the church as one who does and teaches what is the Lord's (Williams 1956a, 44). Origen (c. 185–c. 254) succeeded Clement as head of the catechetical school in Alexandria and made Clement's adult study group into the upper-level theological school of a church-supervised

school. Clement and Origen were among the last of the relatively autonomous teachers in the church. Origen's students worked hard on biblical
interpretation and the study of philosophy. Origen was insistent that the
teacher's task included reinterpreting scripture and tradition in ways that
make sense to contemporary people. Impressed with the difficulty of understanding the meaning of the scriptures correctly, Origen insisted that his
students "tackle the question of how they should be read and understood"
(Origen, 138). Typical of his way of doing this is his comment on the
commandment that forbade the Israelites to eat yesterday's meal. What this
really means, said Origen, is that the teachers of the church ought "not to
set forth stale doctrines according to the letter, but by God's grace ever to
bring forth new truth, ever to discover the spiritual lessons" (cited in Williams 1956a, 47).

The bishops of the early church used every imaginable form of teaching, or so it seems when we look back at their literature. Sermons were
often significant statements on complex doctrinal matters, addressed to
congregations who presumably thought it worth their while to listen to
them. Letters were an important mode of teaching, and many books from
the teachers of the church were sent initially as letters on topics to people
who had requested them. Tertullian wrote many tracts or short books on a
variety of topics as a way of educating the church in Carthage. Many of
the bishops of the church lectured on topics, particularly to baptismal
candidates. Cyril of Jerusalem (c. 315–386) gave addresses on the sacraments that still provide some of the best descriptions of the sacramental
life of the early church, and Gregory of Nyssa (c. 330–395) gave lectures
to baptismal candidates that provide insight into the thinking of a major
figure involved in the trinitarian controversy.

Without belaboring the point or looking at the teaching activity of
everyone known from the ancient church, we need to note that the chief
task of the church in this period of its history was finding its own identity.
Related to, but obviously different from, the Judaism in which it was
born, and even more obviously different from the various mystery religions and cults by which it was surrounded, the church had to work out
its own self-understanding amid persecution from Rome without, and
conflict from within itself. Many of the more discerning leaders of the
church saw the chief heresies of the time as representing little more than
the camel's nose under the tent—the external enemy posing as the internal friend. What helped pull the church through this most difficult period
of its history was the thinking that formed its understanding of God and
the good news of God made available in Jesus Christ and the teaching

activity of the church in which this understanding was worked out. Without claiming that the church always got everything right, which it patently did not, we can nonetheless note with due appreciation the importance it placed on understanding the Christian faith appropriately and teaching it accordingly. We can only wonder that the church in our time can rest so securely in its identity that it does not see the need of undertaking the same tasks today.

Before we leave the early church, let us take a brief look at what some of its foremost teachers had to say on the subject of teaching itself. Gregory of Nazianzus (329–389) was the son of the bishop of Nazianzus in Cappadocia and one of the "Cappadocian fathers" who helped the Nicene faith win out in its struggle with Arianism (the view that the Son of God, incarnate in Jesus Christ, was a creature and not co-eternal with God). Having lived through the period of turmoil in the church following the Council of Nicaea (325), Gregory was keenly aware that "anarchy and disorder" were not advantageous to the church and that "pastors and teachers" were necessary "for the perfecting of the church" (Gregory of Nazianzus, 205). Also, he was leery of being ordained to the office of ministry because of fears of his own inadequacy as well as disregard for some of the holders of the office, of whom he "was ashamed" because "with unwashed hands and uninitiated souls [they] intrude into the most sacred offices," not recognizing that this is "a ministry of which we must give account" (Gregory of Nazianzus, 206). Authoritative as they must be, teachers of the faith are not to be authoritarian nor to presume to be above criticism. This is an important point for the church today, because fear of authoritarianism itself is one of the main obstacles to an authoritative but nonauthoritarian teaching of the faith. Teachers of the faith, presbyters and bishops, must themselves be wise and knowledgeable; it is a great evil "to charge with the instruction of others a man who is not even aware of his own ignorance" (Gregory of Nazianzus, 215). The flock of God is to be fed "with knowledge, not with the instruments of a foolish shepherd" (Gregory of Nazianzus, 227).

Another of the important teachers of the church, John Chrysostom (c. 347–c. 407), in his *Six Books on the Priesthood*, had much to say about teaching the Christian faith. Playing on the word "doctor" (*docere*, to teach), Chrysostom compares the teacher of the Christian faith to a medical doctor. Whereas the latter sometimes prescribes medicines or a change of climate or a good sleep, the doctor of faith finds "only one means and only one method of treatment available, and that is teaching by word of mouth" (Chrysostom, 115). Morality can be taught by providing an example to emulate, but when the soul is suffering from an attack of confusion "words are urgently needed, not only for the safety of the Church's members, but to meet the attacks of outsiders as well" (Chrysostom, 115). Teachers should not use their authority to silence those with whom they disagree lest they acquire "a reputation for arrogance and ignorance" (Chrysostom, 119). Parish priests, the local pastors, are included among those who are commanded to be ready to give an answer (see 1 Peter 3:15). If pastors teach properly, they will build up the church and "lead their disciples, both by what they do and what they say, into the way of that blessed life which Christ commanded. Example alone is not sufficient instruction" (Chrysostom, 125). There were many occasions for teaching in the church, according to Chrysostom, and he took advantage of all of them. For Chrysostom, the bishop was "pre-eminently a teacher and preacher" (Williams 1956b, 70). But preachers are never to forget that if their preaching "does not produce the kind of teaching which is 'with grace, seasoned with salt' " or if they seek applause and speak more for the pleasure than for the profit of their hearers, they fail to do the one thing that they are given and called to do (Chrysostom, 128).

The last writer from the early church we will consider is Gregory the Great (c. 540–604), who was pope from 590 and the last of the traditional Western "Doctors of the Church." His *Book of Pastoral Rule* sets forth the pastoral life and responsibilities of a bishop. Gregory was concerned with all the tasks of a bishop, but throughout the work he speaks of the bishop as a teacher, a physician of souls. Calling the office of bishop "the citadel of teaching," Gregory understands that it is primarily through teaching that the church is governed (Gregory the Great, 1). Shepherds cannot lead the flock without understanding; the blind cannot lead the blind. Gregory knows that the office of bishop (or any pastoral office for that matter) is one in which a person can be pulled in many directions at once. He advises teachers of the Christian faith not to meddle with many matters because the mind cannot be "collected on the plan of any single work while parted among divers" (Gregory the Great, 3). Gregory gives lots of helpful advice to would-be teachers of the Christian faith, one of the more important items of which is not to set one's heart on pleasing people but to pay attention to what *ought* to please them, the gospel of Jesus Christ. Knowing that one is the recipient of God's unbounded love *ought* to please people; one's task is not to become beloved by the people of the parish, but to get the people of the parish to love God and their neighbors (Gregory the Great, 19). The good teacher "ought to study to be loved to the end that he may be listened to, and still not seek love for its own sake" (Gregory the Great, 20). Throughout this book Gregory is insistent that the scriptures and the tradition need to be understood by people, not just recited. Those who do not understand scripture must "consider that they turn for themselves a most wholesome draught of wine into a cup of poison" (Gregory the Great, 51). Hence the Christian faith is to be taught in a way appropriate to the gospel, intelligibly and morally plausible, and with pastoral wisdom and insight in addressing a wide variety of types of people. That is still a fine way to understand the task of the teacher of the Christian faith today, even if we disagree with Chrysostom, as often we must, on what exactly it is that is appropriate, credible, and morally plausible.

Teaching in the Medieval Church

Obviously bishops of the early church like Ambrose and Augustine exemplified the teaching role of the leaders of the church, serving as instructors of the people from the pulpit, engaging in debates, convening councils to discuss difficult issues, arguing even with emperors about matters of public policy, and writing extensively on pressing questions. Augustine devoted Book Four of his *On Christian Doctrine* to preaching, arguing that the purpose of preaching is to teach the Christian faith. He stated the organizing principle of the whole of his book as follows: "There are two things necessary to the treatment of the Scriptures: a way of discovering those things which are to be understood, and a way of teaching what we have learned" (Augustine, 7).

But bishops were never the sole teachers of the Christian faith in their dioceses. Throughout the Middle Ages the parish pastor was the instructor of the people from the pulpit and, ideally, a skilled theologian. The parish priest was the most educated person in the community and people turned to the priest "as counselor, teacher, lawyer, doctor, and friend" (Bainton, 96). Monks in monasteries worked at the training of children, and cathedral churches had their schools for educating children. Indeed, public education in the Middle Ages, such as it was, was largely carried out by churches. In the fifth century, after the "barbarian" invasions, "there were no schools in Gaul and Africa; . . . education had been dealt a severe blow" (Deanesly, 32). The tradition of sending boys to the bishop for education began to take form. The duty of teaching young "clerks" shifted by the eighth century from bishops to presbyters (Deanesly, 33). In the eighth century, under Charlemagne, Alcuin (c. 735–c. 804) presided over a revival of classical and biblical learning that has been called the "Carolingian Renaissance." Charlemagne himself occasionally was a pupil in the palace school; under his and Alcuin's leadership learning grew and theological discussion of the meaning of the Christian faith intensified. At the same time the reform efforts of Chrodegang of Metz required a sermon to be preached every two weeks, preferably one that is "careful," that the people can understand (Deanesly, 58). The educational work of cathedral and monastic schools throughout the Middle Ages, as well as that of monastic orders such as the Dominicans, can be said to have educated Europe. The revival of learning in the tenth and eleventh centuries led to translating the Gospels into Anglo-Saxon, as well as to preaching in local languages and providing translations of the scriptures in services of worship (Deanesly, 99). Concern with translation is concern with intelligibility, with being understood by the people. Throughout the Middle Ages, both the regular, faithful service of the church by its clergy and the repeated attempts at reform focused on the need for an educated clergy who could teach the Christian faith.

Teaching in the Reformation

Although teaching was always considered an essential part of the minister's task, whether that minister was a bishop or a local pastor, the Reformation provides the basis for that understanding of teaching as ministry that mainline churches today need most to recapture. We shall begin with Martin Luther. In his thought, as well as that of John Calvin and John Wesley, we find "understandings of the teaching office that point toward a non-authoritarian style of teaching authority in the church" (Osmer, 2). The Reformers held that the church is to teach its faith with real authority, but that this authority was neither that of an infallible pope nor that of a free-lance magnetic leader operating outside the norms of the Christian faith. This nonhierarchical, nonauthoritarian, yet not merely individualistic understanding of teaching authority that we inherit from the Reformation is best described as a dialogical or conversational understanding of teaching. As mainline churches grapple with the question of how they are to teach the Christian faith today, "they would do well to retrieve the heritage of the teaching office as it is found in the thought of the great Reformers" (Osmer, 5).

Luther's first rule for good preaching was this: "First of all, a good preacher must be able to teach correctly and in an orderly manner. Second, he must have a good head. Third, he must be able to speak well. Fourth, he should have a good voice, and, fifth, a good memory. Sixth, he must know when to stop. Seventh, he must know his stuff and keep at it" (cited in Pauck, 134). Luther's understanding of the church's teaching

authority is that it is based on the authority of scripture *as* scripture witnesses to the gospel. At the core of his and Calvin's thought "was an
affirmation of the absolute priority of the gospel" (Osmer, 16). The good
news of God's love graciously disclosed in Jesus Christ is the gospel that
teaches us who God is and who we are in relation to God and one another, and who Jesus Christ is as the one through whom we come to learn
who God and we are. The gospel is the "authority above all authorities in
the church, the foundation upon which all others rest" (Osmer, 17). Scripture itself cannot be used in an authoritarian way, for example, because it
points beyond itself to Jesus Christ as *rex scripturae*, "king of scripture."
The teaching office of the church, in turn, also stands under the gospel as
disclosed in the scriptures; what is taught in church, no matter who is
doing the teaching, must be assessed by reference to the critical principle
of the gospel. It was this authoritative yet nonauthoritarian understanding
of the teaching function of the church that brought the Reformers into
conflict with the teaching office as it was understood in the medieval
church because, according to the Reformers, the medieval church set itself
above scripture and the gospel in determining the essentials of Christian
faith and life. Challenging medieval understandings of the infallibility of
the church, Calvin argued:

> If we grant . . . that the church cannot err in matters necessary to salvation,
> here is what we mean by it: The statement is true in so far as the church,
> having forsaken all its own wisdom, allows itself to be taught by the Holy
> Spirit through God's Word. This, then, is the difference. Our opponents
> locate the authority of the church outside God's Word; but we insist that it
> be attached to the Word, and do not allow it to be separated from it (Calvin,
> 1162).

Calvin, more than Luther, developed the understanding of the teaching office of the church (see Goodykoontz, 46–75). In his discussion of the
ministry in the *Institutes,* Calvin holds that every pastor is to be a teacher
of the faith. The church is governed by the word, particularly by the
preaching and teaching of the word: "nothing fosters mutual love more
fittingly than for men to be bound together with this bond: one is appointed pastor to teach the rest" (Calvin, 1054). The "renewal of the
saints is accomplished . . . [and] the body of Christ is built up" through
the teaching ministry of the church. Calvin regarded the apostles,
prophets, and evangelists of the ministry of the early church (Eph. 4:11)
as temporary functions of the church. The twelve apostles and Paul were
gracious gifts to the church, but we no longer have apostles; the class of
prophets "does not exist today or is less commonly seen" (Calvin, 1057).

Evangelists were people close to the apostles and younger than they, such as Luke, Timothy, and Titus. The permanent offices of the church, which the church can never do without, are pastors and teachers.

Calvin understood that every pastor is a teacher, but that every teacher need not also be a pastor (Henderson, 31). As "teachers correspond to the ancient prophets, so do our pastors to the apostles" (Calvin, 1058). Pastors are to preach and administer the sacraments and to teach, and teaching involves not only understanding the content of the Christian faith but instructing people in what it means to live new and transformed lives, what Calvin called instruction in "true godliness" (Calvin, 1059). In the form of church government that Calvin submitted to the city council of Geneva, and that was adopted, provision was made for four church offices: preachers, teachers, elders, and deacons (Pauck, 129). Calvin thought (of course!) that this form of church government was definitely prescribed by the New Testament. The pastors in Geneva were organized collegially and so functioned (and do until this day). Their task was to preach, teach, administer the sacraments, and oversee the discipline of the church, in which task they were joined by the elders. Teachers as a separate office taught in the Academy, a theological school for the education of people for the ministry. Deacons administered poor relief and charities. The Reformer John Knox referred to Geneva under Calvin as "the greatest school of Christ on earth" (Pauck, 130).

Probably it was because of the insistence on teaching as a critical component of the pastor's task that teaching became so important throughout the Reformation churches. Catechisms (question-and-answer books summarizing the chief articles of the Christian faith) were introduced everywhere and provided the foundation for pastoral teaching. Typically, after the sermon the pastor would lead the congregation in reciting the catechism or parts of it. Preaching itself sought to convey an appropriate understanding of the Christian faith, of the teachings of the gospel, not to stimulate conversion experiences or to manipulate the moods and feelings of congregants. Reformation preachers were primarily teachers. The sacraments, when they were administered, were usually accompanied by teaching, explaining what is happening (Pauck, 135).

It is important to mainline churches today to notice that Luther and Calvin supported what we earlier called a conversational model of the teaching office: "No single authority can lay exclusive claim to the definitive conservation and interpretation of scripture" (Osmer, 20). Rather, there are several less-than-ultimate authorities, all finite and fallible (Henderson, 246) and all involved in an unending process of conversation and interpretation, and these authorities constitute the teaching authority of the church. For example, Luther and Calvin both held church councils as teaching authorities, authorities that, like others, were fallible and subject to the critical principle of the gospel. Also, both held that the church could gather groups of representative Christians to provide ongoing guidance to Christians on matters of moral and social importance. Further, both Luther and Calvin thought that the ongoing work of theologians was a source of teaching authority, as theologians undertook the task to criticize the witness of the church in the light of the norms of the faith. Since the Reformation began in a theologian's study at Wittenberg, the Reformers valued the freedom of theologians from church supervision while regarding theologians, too, as fallible and needing to participate in further conversation with other centers of Christian teaching. The congregation was a source of teaching authority and had the responsibility to test the teachings of pastors, teachers, and theologians; like them, however, its authority is not absolute and must be entertained only in conversation with others. One wonders why we are not moved to recreate in today's church something analogous to this pluralistic, nonauthoritarian style of teaching invented by the Reformers. As Calvin would have it, pastors are to teach and teachers are to function in a way that is "didactic and critical in contradistinction to the liturgical, shepherding, and governing competence of the apostolic-pastoral office" (Henderson, 31). It is something of a mystery that these two teaching functions have almost completely disappeared.

The Schoolmaster in the School

From the seventeenth century, we have a marvelous example of Calvin's understanding of the pastor-teacher from the pen of Richard Baxter (1615–1691), a Puritan pastor. Baxter thought of the "reformed" pastor not as a Protestant pastor but as one "called to faithful service" (Baxter, 10). His claim, then, is one upon which we still place *some* hope: "If God would but reform the ministry, and set them on their duties zealously and faithfully, the People would certainly be reformed" (Baxter, 10). Baxter's book consists mainly of helpful, practical advice to those who would be such faithful pastors.

Baxter tells of how the Puritan clergy in his county in England were "awakened . . . to a sense of their duty in the work of catechizing and private instruction of *all* in their parishes" (Baxter, 13). Convinced that all Christians should know and understand the Christian faith, Baxter felt it a poor discharge of the pastor's duty "if there be a thousand or five hundred ignorant people in your parish" for the pastor only "occasionally to speak to some few of them and let the rest alone in their ignorance" (Baxter, 18). So he (and other pastors as well) organized the parish into small groups of fifteen to sixteen families and met with each group once a week, "that we may go through the parish, which hath above eight hundred families, in a year" (Baxter, 19).

The clergy themselves were not regarded as an authoritarian, infallible group of people but, instead, as in need of being taught, admonished, and exhorted by each other on a regular basis (Baxter, 25). Baxter took as his text Paul's address to the elders of the church in Ephesus as reported in Acts 20:28: "Take heed to yourselves and to all the flock, in which the Holy Spirit has made you overseers, to care for the church of God which he obtained with the blood of his own Son." The word "overseers" is *episkopous*, "guardians" or "bishops." Baxter, in the Reformed tradition, regards them as "officers appointed to teach and guide those Churches in the way to salvation, and it is the same persons that are called elders at the Church of Ephesus before, and bishops here" (Baxter, 26). They were parish pastors (Baxter, 27).

Parish pastors were to "take heed," first, to themselves, and with God's help to seek to preach and teach the Christian faith with integrity. Those who preach saving grace should ask whether that same grace has worked its way in their own souls (Baxter, 28), lest they be living contradictions of their own proclamation. Yet pastors cannot be content with being open to God's grace; they must also preach their sermons to themselves before they preach them to others: "When I let my heart grow cold, my preaching is cold; and when it is confused, my preaching will be so; and so I can observe too oft in the best of my hearers, that when I have a while grown cold in preaching, they have cooled accordingly" (Baxter, 33). Also, pastors should take heed lest their example contradict their doctrine "and lest you lay such stumbling blocks before the blind as may be the occasion of their ruin: lest you unsay with your lives what you say with your tongues" (Baxter, 34). Yet Baxter thinks that pastors also ought to ask themselves how ready they are to *teach* the Christian faith:

> He must not himself be a babe in knowledge that will teach men all those mysterious things that are to be known in order to salvation. Oh what qualifications are necessary for a man who hath such a charge upon him as we have! How many difficulties in divinity to be opened; and these too about the very fundamentals that must needs be known. How many obscure texts of Scripture to be expounded (Baxter, 37).

Consequently, Baxter placed a high value on continuing study by the clergy: "It is too common with us to be negligent in our studies. Few men are at the pains that are necessary for the right informing of their understanding and fitting them for further work. . . . Many ministers study only to compose their sermons and very little more, when there are so many books to be read and so many matters that we should not be unacquainted with" (Baxter, 96).

What the pastor is charged with is being the guardian or overseer of the flock. *How* the pastor carries out this oversight is by teaching. Pastors are to seek to "convert the unconverted" by teaching them who God is, who they are, and who Jesus Christ is. Pastors are to be ready to provide advice to parishioners who come to them with questions of conscience. Pastors are to work for the "building up of those that are already converted" (Baxter, 53). Pastors are to have "a special eye upon families, to see that they be well ordered" (Baxter, 58).

The teaching pastor should "insist upon the greatest, most certain, and most necessary truths, and be more seldom and sparing upon the rest" (Baxter, 72). Teaching should be "as plain and evident as we can make it" (Baxter, 72). And we should "so teach others as to be ready to learn of any that can teach us" (Baxter, 73). All of this must be carried on "in a tender love to our people" (Baxter, 75). Our teaching must always bear witness to "the unity and peace of the whole Church" (Baxter, 99).

What Baxter insisted on most heavily, however, was the duty of the pastor to engage in "personal catechizing and instructing every one in your parishes or congregations that will submit thereto" (Baxter, 104). Parishioners who understand the Christian faith better will "make our public preaching to be better understood and regarded" (Baxter, 108). "The minister is in the church," said Baxter, "as the schoolmaster is in his school, to teach and take account of every one in particular, and that all Christians ordinarily must be disciples or scholars in some such school" (Baxter, 111).

The Pastor-Teacher

In our time, Wesner Fallaw developed an understanding of ministry very much like Baxter's. Indeed, Fallaw's concept of "church education" might be thought of as an updated version of Baxter's argument. Like Baxter, Fallaw would make of the pastor the chief teacher of the Christian faith in the congregation. "Ours," he declares, "is a faith to be taught, and taught with all the competency we can summon" (Fallaw, 10). The chief difficulty in the way of this, as Fallaw sees it, is that the tasks of people in the congregation are inappropriately distributed. Those with the most theological education and therefore the greatest ability for teaching the Christian faith do not do so. Those without a theological education and therefore without the capacity for teaching the Christian faith in a reflective and sustained way are the ones who get the job. What Fallaw urges upon the clergy is not yet more responsibilities but more appropriate ones, with the less appropriate jobs reassigned to others (Fallaw, 11). Let the pastor become the chief teacher of the Christian faith in the congregation and assign responsibility for administration, for example, to lay people. They are probably better at it anyway, and this would free pastors for the "full exercise of their calling, their training and abilities" (Fallaw, 11).

Fallaw's proposal calls for a radical overhaul of the way ministry is done in the local church. The Sunday school would be replaced with "church education" (Fallaw, 13). Most of the teaching would be done by the pastor—the one best prepared to do it. Lay people would not be used less in church education, just *misused* less. Their role in the teaching of classes would be to run interest groups, field trips, and workshops. They could work as assistants, oversee lesson preparation, handle audiovisual aids, direct projects and dramatics, and so on (Fallaw, 58). The pastor would teach the class, and every class in the church, at times scheduled throughout the week. Convinced that "teaching in the church belongs on a par with preaching" (Fallaw, 21), we cannot avoid the idea that the primary responsibility for classroom teaching of the Christian faith belongs to the theologically educated pastor, a pastor who must also be competent in education (Fallaw, 70–90).

Not only does Fallaw propose a complete overhaul of the structure of education in the church, he also broaches a curriculum for church education, one which breaks out of the bibliocentric orientation characteristic of many church curricula. Fallaw would have the pastor-teacher utilize her or his theological education and actually teach classes in church history, ethics, theology, critical biblical studies, and comparative religion, among other topics (Fallaw, 148–149). What Fallaw proposes is nothing short of making the church into the schoolhouse of Christians, much as the synagogue is the school of the Jewish faith.

Furthermore, what Fallaw sets forth is not merely an idealization of what might be. Along the way he meets every possible objection of the "it can't be done" variety and shows how it can. He offers many concrete suggestions that are helpful in making it possible for the church to engage in serious education in the Christian faith. Throughout, his stress is both on the importance of education in the faith and on the role of the pastor as the chief (not the only) teacher of the Christian faith in the congregation.

In his *The Purpose of the Church and Its Ministry*, H. Richard Niebuhr articulated the role of the minister as that of the "pastoral director" (Niebuhr, 79ff.). This description has often been taken to mean that Niebuhr was arguing for the minister's function to be comprised of equal parts of pastor and administrator ("director"). But this was not his intent, even though the name "pastoral director" may have been, in retrospect, an unhappy choice. Rather, claimed Niebuhr, the pastor's "first function is that of building or 'edifying' the church; he is concerned in everything that he does to bring into being a people of God who as a Church will serve the purpose of the Church in the local community and the world" (Niebuhr, 82). Preaching, for example, is to be directed "toward the *instruction*, the persuasion, the counseling of persons who are becoming members of the body of Christ and who are carrying on the mission of the Church" (Niebuhr, 82). Preaching should help Christian people grow into mature adulthood "in the measure of the stature of the fullness of Christ" and enable them "to interpret to others the meaning of the Christian faith" (Niebuhr, 82). As teacher of the Christian faith, "the pastoral director becomes the teacher of teachers, the head of all educational organization which he cannot simply manage but must lead as a competent Christian educator" (Niebuhr, 83). The church is to minister to the needs of the world, and the minister is to serve the church by teaching it, never merely by simply administering whatever programs are demanded or facilitating whatever people might want to do. So to misunderstand Niebuhr is to miss the significance of the theological introduction to his book in which he gives voice to the purpose of the church, which he construes as that of spreading among people the love of God and of the neighbor.

Conclusion

The ministry today is indeed a "perplexed profession." If the mainline churches are to find a way out of their quagmire and rediscover the purpose of the church, the ministry, too, will have to find a way out of its bewilderment into some theological clarity as to its own role. We suggest that it can best do this by reappropriating in our time the model of the pastor-teacher. To re-appropriate this model is to appropriate it anew, not simply to repeat some older way of understanding the function of the pastor-teacher. But there are clues from the tradition that can be helpful. The pastor-teacher will work in a conversational context with other teachers of the Christian faith, not in an individualistic and authoritarian manner. The pastor-teacher will understand his or her task as that of the primary teacher of the Christian faith in a congregation. The pastor-teacher will observe the critical principle of self-questioning on which the accounts given by prophets and apostles lay such emphasis. Pastor-teachers will regularly ask themselves whether the lesson they are conveying is God's word and not simply another word of their own or of the culture (Jenkins, 29). That is, pastor-teachers will have to be good workaday theologians, asking themselves how the Christian witness can be made in such a way that it is appropriate to that to which it claims to bear witness, how it makes sense, and how it is morally plausible.

In our next chapter, we will go more fully into the questions at which we just hint here, questions of the relation between theological reflection and the task of the pastor-teacher. Here we want to stake out the claim that it is in the understanding of the task of the minister as that of the pastor-teacher that the way ahead for the church and ministry can be found, in our time or in any time. Reform and renewal of the church must begin again as they have always begun, in the case of Luther and Calvin for example, with a renewed concern for the authentic teaching of the Christian faith.

4
DOING THEOLOGY:
A NUTS-AND-BOLTS
APPROACH

To recap for a moment, we have looked so far at why the teaching model of ministry is again emerging as important in the life of American mainline churches, at what the relation of teaching to proclamation was in the traditions of Israel and the early church, and at how Christian ministry was always understood to include teaching as one of its core components throughout the history of the church. Finally, in the traditions in which many mainline Protestants stand, we saw teaching emerge both as a distinct office or function within the church and as a critically important component of pastoral ministry and oversight.

At this point in our discussion we turn to the question of the relation between the teaching ministry and the doing of theology. We do this because we suspect that it is precisely at this point that the greatest breakdown occurs in today's churches. Theology, as pastors too often encountered it during their seminary studies, seems to have little or nothing to do with the life of the churches or the people in them, and to be written in any number of highly coded languages which virtually defy translation into recognizable and understandable speech. There is a gulf, in other words, between theology and the church, and the worst part of a gulf is that those on one side of it cannot reach out to those on the other; also there is the distinct possibility that they will not even be acquainted with one another. So it often seems today between theology and the church.

It is precisely this gulf that we seek to bridge. Let us begin with a story, a tale about a deliberative assembly of a mainline church, an assembly that both writers of this book recently attended. At this assembly a number of significant and controversial issues were discussed: a resolution on authority in the church, a report on the meaning of salvation through Jesus Christ, an emergency resolution on abortion rights, resolutions on ecumenical relationships with other churches, and resolutions on a host of social, political, economic, and moral issues. What was striking was not the particular results of the voting on these issues but the character of the discussion.

Take, for example, the resolution on authority in the church. This particular resolution was a statement affirming the authority of the scriptures. Two groups of people debated the resolution, one for and the other against. The affirmative group held a view of biblical authority that was quite narrow and restrictive and that made the rest of the assembly, clearly the majority, feel that the resolution, if passed, would subsequently serve as a club with which to beat down all sorts of good proposals on the grounds that they were not biblical. The negative group, opposed to the resolution, stated their opposition in such a way as to indicate that they could accept *no* authority over themselves in the church and did so on the grounds that all authority they had ever known had been oppressive, authoritarian, and denied the rights and aspirations of women, racial and ethnic minorities, and others.

Neither group discussed the issue of authority theologically, nor made any of the simplest distinctions that might have helped move the conversation along. Rather, we had a nontheological discussion on both sides of the issue as to whether the church recognizes scripture as authoritative. The discussion disclosed, however, that the two opposing groups manage to live together in an unhealthy symbiosis, each frightening and reinforcing the other. The narrow and restrictive group, with its closed-off style of ·authority and identity, strikes the "liberals" as authoritarian and oppressive. The wide-open group strikes the "conservatives" as boundaryless and normless, as representing an "anything goes" mentality in the church. Neither group presented *theological* arguments about a matter of central importance in the church.

This incident confirms the analysis of the plight of the mainline churches laid out in our first chapter and indicates how crucial it is to those churches to acquire once again the ability to think theologically about the meaning of the Christian faith. It is to this task, specifically to the question of how to go about doing just that—thinking theologically—that we now turn.

Retrieving the Tradition

Given the analyses of the plight of the mainline churches that we outlined in the first chapter, it is not surprising that a number of people have gone on record to the effect that the churches must recover their capacity to think theologically. Nor should we be astonished to discover that they have spelled out how the churches should do this. Thomas Oden, who teaches theology at Drew University, has made a significant proposal in this regard, one that we discuss here under the heading "Retrieving the Tradition." We call it that because of Oden's thesis: "Everything required for the future care of American Protestantism has already been providentially offered as consensually received instruction in classical Christian writings" (Oden, 72). Oden understands himself to be setting forth a "postmodern ortho-doxy," an understanding of Christian faith that does *not* seek to come to terms with the crises of modernity, those radical questions posed by mod-ern science and Enlightenment morality. The mainline churches have too much sought to come to terms with "the world," Oden would doubtless say, with the result that they can now hardly distinguish themselves from it. So what we should do, instead, is try to show that *everything* necessary to the vitality of the church is available in "centrist classical sources" from *before* the year 1700 (Oden, 72). Only obedience to the classical ecumenical consensus of Christian theology can deliver contemporary Protestantism from the "incipient narcissisms, pantheisms, atheisms, naturalisms, modern messianisms, and failed (but still constantly touted) social and political stratagems" (Oden, 73).

Oden's method is to state a series of propositions (forty-seven in all) and then to cite in behalf of each a passage from the ancient consensus that, in effect, argues for that proposition. Obviously, Oden's forty-seven propositions constitute more claims and arguments than can be accounted for here. He is far from trying to be stiflingly "traditional"; instead, he has been said to be trying to bring about "liberation by tradition" (Stall-sworth, 144). We may take his theses about women as an instance. "Women are destined," maintains Oden, "to play a crucial, and perhaps the decisive, role in the third millenium of Christianity" (Oden, 90). Fur-ther: "The church earnestly prays for the right calling, inspiring, and ful-fillment of prophetic gifts of women amid our present crisis" (Oden, 91). From the tradition Oden also adduces arguments for the courage of women (so needed in the present crisis that the church faces) and for their right to teach in the church. Oden contends for other points as well, with many of which we find ourselves in agreement. His emphases on the proper functioning of the ministry of the church—its concern with teach-ing the Christian faith, with proper and more rigorous attention to ques-tions of ordination and standing in relation to such questions—are quite in line with suggestions we have made here about teaching the Christian faith.

Nonetheless, Oden's approach leaves us uneasy. As people who have taken responsibility for teaching historical theology in a seminary, we are aware that the classical tradition is a rich and broad stream and that there are within it many forgotten alternatives, possibilities that have their pertinence to today's questions. To cite one that Oden does not mention, the first argument (by a Christian) of which we are aware that we should call God "parent" and not "father" occurs in an apology *(The Octavius)* written in the late second or early third century (Minucius Felix, 192–194). Yet one could easily make too much of such a bit of knowledge, particularly as nothing came of it; nor would we even think of retrieving such a piece of historical lore today if, in fact, we were not listening to feminist voices and the issues that they raise, a kind of listening for which Oden's proposal does not provide. Nor does Oden point out wherein the ecumenical consensus falls short. In the quotation arguing for the right of women to teach in the church, Oden fails to note that it authorizes "well instructed" women "to be able aptly and properly to teach unskilled and rustic women how to answer at the time of their baptism the questions put to them" (Oden, 92). That is, women may teach other women, but not, apparently, men. The women who do the teaching must themselves be well instructed. By whom? Oden does admit that although God has always called women, nonetheless their calling now to enter the ministry "is a new appropriation of what I understand to be the original deposit of faith that has indeed been *misunderstood for nineteen centuries*" (Oden, 142; emphasis ours).

Just here lies the problem for Oden's claim as to how we ought to do theology in the mainline churches today. His concern with the impressionability or malleability of the mainline churches, the way they seem so often to be putty in the hands of the world, their willingness to be persuaded out of a desire to be "sensitive," all suggest to Oden that the only way ahead is backward—to the tradition. One can understand why Oden thinks so, and one must recognize that there is more in the tradition than the churches have even begun to appropriate. Knowledge of it would indeed provide some perspective on the present situation.

Oden, however, claims too much in declaring that all our future theological needs are provided for in the pre-1700 centrist writings of the church. Were he to go so far as to include some of the noncentrist writings (by women, for example), his point would be a little stronger but still insufficient. The reasons for this are several: (1) We cannot avoid the crisis of authority, including the authority of tradition, by retreating to the premodern world; however much we find wrong with the modern world (and we should find quite a lot because it gave us Auschwitz and Hiroshima), we cannot go back behind it. (2) We cannot overlook the fact that much of what is wrong with the contemporary church in fact stems from a (perhaps uncritical) continuation of traditional stances and attitudes. With regard to how Jews and women are regarded and treated, for example, most Christians are incredibly traditional; the numbers of Christians who have been influenced by post-Holocaust, post-Vatican II statements on Jews, for example, is minuscule. In other words, Oden does not recognize how deeply flawed the tradition is, nor does he give us a way to deal with the fact that it is, since he views the tradition as the only remedy for our situation. (3) Therefore we need not only to retrieve the tradition as a resource for dealing with the present, and to criticize it in the light of that to which it would witness, but we need the freedom to think anew and act anew, in ways not approved by the tradition. After all, if the tradition misunderstood that the call and claim of God are extended to women as well as men, and maintained that misunderstanding for nineteen centuries, we might as well admit that we have some new thoughts on such matters today, and feel free to entertain them. *Semper reformanda* is also a tradition. Oden is correct in his assumption that the church is too unaware of its tradition. It is also true, however, that the church can be too much steeped in its tradition, trapped within its perspectives. The one alternative is as dangerous as the other. Recognizing the strengths and the weaknesses of Oden's recommendation, we suggest instead a modification of it: that the mainline churches learn again how to conduct a conversation with the Christian tradition, how to retrieve it critically.

A Critical Orthodoxy

Another response to the crisis of theology in today's mainline churches has been prepared by John H. Leith, a Presbyterian scholar who has written and edited several books on the Christian tradition. Addressing himself directly to the decline in the Presbyterian Church (U.S.A.), Leith analyzes both membership loss and the leadership/laity split in this church. He notices, for instance, this:

> The activity of Presbyterians in political life presents a strange anomaly. Never before have the Presbyterian General Assemblies and the various staffs of the church been so prolific in turning out political, social, and economic pronouncements and in the funding of political advocacy organizations. This political activity has generally been in agreement with the political positions of the left wing of the Democratic Party. Yet the last significant political action in which Presbyterians engaged was the election of Ronald Reagan (Leith, 12).

The decline and the gap between leaders and followers reflect a more basic crisis: "the loss of the theological integrity and competence of the church's witness, in particular in preaching, teaching, and pastoral care" (Leith, 13). Renewal will not come without their recovery, nor without a revitalization of preaching. The church must recognize that any expertise it may have in matters of therapy, sociology, economics, and politics is strictly "derivative"; it "grows out of biblical and theological wisdom as well as out of commitment to the God and Father of our Lord Jesus Christ" (Leith, 14).

Chiefly influenced by the Reformed (Calvinist) tradition in theology and the neo-orthodox giants, Leith insists that the church's credibility "in any field" turns upon "the credibility of the faith commitment and on the theological wisdom that is evident in the church's life" (Leith, 14). Hence the renewal of theology and of theological preaching is essential. The chief source of the church's malaise is "the loss of a distinctive Christian message and of the theological and biblical competence that made its preaching effective" (Leith, 22). Needed is preaching that both proclaims the gospel, calling sinners to repentance and faith, and does so intelligibly because faith seeks intelligibility, "the intelligibility of the faith itself and of human existence in the world in the light of that faith. This is the intellectual task of preaching" (Leith, 23).

Because preaching was taken as seriously as it was in the Reformation (lively preaching of the gospel *is* the word of God), these movements have much to teach us about preaching today. What they have to teach us makes the task clearer and simpler, if not easier. First, the Calvinist movement advocated plain-style preaching: "Calvin spoke in plain language, and he intended the message to be the medium" (Leith, 26). What Calvin valued most in preaching was clarity, directness, and authenticity; what he abominated was everything pompous, pretentious, artificial, and contrived. The straightforward, direct witness to the gospel of Jesus Christ can be trusted to make its own impact; preachers are to call attention to the message they bear, not to themselves.

Second, Reformation-style preaching stands in the closest relationship to Christian education or Christian nurture, what we prefer to call "theological education in the church." As Leith states it: "The content of the Calvinist sermon is directed toward those who have reflected on the Christian faith" (Leith, 27). Such reflection—critical thinking—is what the Calvinist tradition means by "discipline." Hence: "Calvinist worship requires a disciplined congregation" (Leith, 27). Thinking theologically about the Christian faith both helps the congregation to "hear" the sermon and to live out the Christian faith.

Readers will have noticed that we started out talking about theology and how it should be done and moved, very quickly, into a discussion about the life of the church, particularly about the lively preaching, teaching, and learning of the Christian faith. We did this to show that theological reflection is no alienated enterprise but essential to the church when the church itself is set upon its own purpose, that of witnessing to the gospel of God's all-inclusive, freely given love and carrying out God's command that justice be done to all of those whom God loves. What Leith so helpfully contends is that if the church is in the service of its central purpose it must develop a "critical orthodoxy," one in which the church is clear about its own identity and then (and only then) able to allow contemporary questions and knowledge to inform and deepen its witness (Leith, 37). Standing within the tradition, the church can carry on a conversation with "the world outside the church" (Leith, 38). Its character and perhaps its existence *as* church is endangered, however, when those inside speak as if they were outside the church, if they engage in what Peter Berger called "secularization from within." To engage in a genuine conversation with the world is very different from seeking to bring the church into line with the world.

Such a conversation requires the church to make a witness that is singularly its own (one that is appropriate to the Christian faith), at the same time that it requires the church to make this witness credibly (Leith, 40). Faith seeks understanding, intelligibility. Faith claims to be true, not just one option among many. While this does not mean that we can "prove" the Christian faith to be true, says Leith, nonetheless there are various proximate steps we can take and public tests we can make by which faith can be distinguished from mere infatuation. We can show the internal coherence of the faith (clarify its logic), show its adequacy in dealing with such universal human crises as death, demonstrate its fruits in the lives of Christian communities and individuals, point out that it has found credence among people "under different conditions and in many times and places" (Leith, 40), indicate its communitarian character (it's not just my idiosyncrasy), and illustrate its power to "illuminate human experience" (Leith, 40). "Faith does not seek demonstration or proof but intelligibility, the intelligibility of the faith itself and the intelligibility of the world and human experience in the light of the faith" (Leith, 40).

The difference between Leith's proposal and Oden's is that Leith would not limit theological development to the years before 1700. He would both allow and encourage a conversation with the contemporary situation. Let us take these two points in reverse order. Oden's way of handling the boundarylessness of the mainstream is to close the door against even the prospect of a conversation with the situation—we'll just dance with the theological tradition that brought us to the beginning of the modern world, thank you very much. Leith's proposal allows and requires the church to learn from and be willing to accept criticism from the contemporary situation *if* the church already knows its own identity, what is given to and required of it to say *to* the situation in which it finds itself. A proper understanding of the church yields a proper openness to the world. One reason we think Leith's proposal important is that we regard the openness of the mainline churches to the culture to be both their greatest weakness and their greatest strength. The dual lesson we pointed out in the first chapter is that while these churches suffer from overidentification with the culture, the answer to their troubles is not to be found in a withdrawal into a closed-off, restrictive style of church life. Rather, it is to be found in a genuine (two-way) conversation with the culture (or the "situation") in which the church participates as one who has something to say as well as something to hear. We think this is a more adequate, if more difficult, stance than Oden's.

In that sense Leith's position is more radical than Oden's, more open to change. Yet we might well ask how open to change, to transformation, is it? Leith himself says that one of the most important things he ever learned theologically is "the law of *minimal* theological development" (Leith, 15; emphasis ours). His book reflects his commitment to this principle. It is a fine articulation of how the church should understand itself and bear its witness in the light of the Catholic and Reformed traditions up through the era of Karl Barth, William Temple, and the Niebuhrs. Important as these thinkers are, an importance we by no means gainsay, it is odd that a late-1980s book on theological revitalization within the church should not discuss issues arising from the women's movement, from the ecological crisis, from liberation theologies, from radical theologies, or from African-American theologies. Yet, attention to such questions would call for more than *minimal* theological development.

What have we learned so far? From Oden, we have learned that theology should be appropriate to, but not trapped within, the Christian tradition. From Leith, we have learned that theology should help the church clarify its identity and purpose and understand its faith intelligibly so that it can bear a credible witness. From him we also learn that the church should be in conversation with (neither closed-off against nor uncritically open to) the situation in which it finds itself. We also note that this conversation with the situation and with new theologies arising within the church will require, *contra* Leith, more than a minimal theological development. How do we put all this together in a coherent package, an approach to doing theology that tries to be adequate to the task without being so complex and cumbersome as to be impossible to achieve? To that question we now turn.

Tradition as Conversation with
Past and Present

In a time when the churches have become uncertain of their identity, theologians understandably turn to tradition as the antidote. Precisely because tradition is important to the church's identity and to the theological task, a clarifying word about how best to understand it should prove useful. The main problem with the term "tradition" is that it is a noun, which leads people to think of tradition as a "thing," indeed an inert thing. Thinking of tradition as an inert thing leads to regarding it as the dead or oppressive hand of the past and something at all costs to be avoided. According to this understanding, it is tradition itself, and specifically the Christian tradition, from which we need to be liberated. Hence we derive the problem of "tradition versus the individual."

We suggest thinking of tradition primarily as a verb, not a noun, as a process, not a thing. The Latin verb *traditio* means "to pass on." The term "traditioning" today has much this same meaning. When we pass on a tradition, which families do when they tell stories from the family history, we also incorporate people into a tradition. Not to be incorporated into a tradition is not to know who you are, to whom you are related, where you come from, or where you are going. That is why the scriptures admonish us: "Remove not the ancient landmark, which your fathers have set" (Prov. 22:28). So, to "tradition" is to engage in a sociohistorical process. At the same time, one who has attended the same family reunion across a span of years recognizes that the stories and storytellers change, that this very traditional and traditioning activity is literally never the same twice.

Now consider that at whatever point we might look at the community of faith throughout its history we *always* find it in this situation: It has a tradition (or a set of traditions not always easily reconciled with each other) that it inherits and cherishes and it encounters new and unanticipated events that are happening. These events (such as Job's sufferings) may be at odds with the deliverances of the tradition, may seem to deny the sense of the tradition (can the God who promised them a land send the people into exile?), or may be so radically unexpected as simply to astound those who take the tradition seriously.

It is not only the biblical community of faith, however, that we find in such a situation. We also find the church throughout its history and in the present in the same situation, that of receiving a tradition and encountering new situations, a receiving and an encountering that generate conflict between tradition and situation and that *can* also generate creativity. At every point in our historical life the community of faith, as well as the individual Christian, is faced with a hermeneutical task: We have to interpret this new situation in the light of the tradition in order to understand it and to incorporate it into this *living* tradition. Tradition is not a matter of a sentimental attitude toward the past; "in even the very best living tradition there is always a mixture of good and bad, and much that deserves criticism" (Eliot, 19). Looking upon tradition as a sociohistorical process enables us to see how it is as true to say that we have no intelligence without tradition as it is true to say that a tradition without intelligence is not worth having. Living tradition is tradition that is "perpetually criticized and brought up to date under the supervision of . . . orthodoxy" (Eliot, 67). "Orthodoxy" means correct *thinking*, not correct "thought."

Therefore we must reinterpret the tradition if it is to incorporate new developments and to be credible in the face of them. Yet it is also tradition, in this sense, that renders these new developments intelligible, that "makes sense" of them. The tradition remains a living tradition by enabling us to interpret and understand the new situations in which we live and by itself being open to reinterpretation. The more radical the shift in our situations from one generation to the next, the more radical will our reinterpretation of the received tradition have to be. It is precisely because new interpretations of tradition are as creative and diverse as they are that we need to take care that our new interpretations are themselves, however creative, appropriate to the Christian faith. That an interpretation is new is not in itself evidence that it is proper or fitting. For example, the "German Christians" who supported Hitler offered new, but not therefore suitable, interpretations of the Christian faith.

Every time pastors step into the pulpit, teach a class, speak to a group in the church, or in any way make the Christian witness to people, they reinterpret the Christian tradition. On every such occasion a pastor stands in the Christian tradition and faces people living in the contemporary situation. The task before the pastor is to enable these people to understand their situation in the light of the Christian tradition—the Christian faith as it has been mediated to them—and to understand the Christian faith in a way appropriate to their situation. Our new understandings or interpretations must be appropriate to the Christian faith and relevant to the situation. Like it or not, pastors are always involved in the act of reinterpreting the Christian tradition. They are neither simply passing it on unchanged nor are they able to speak from a position outside or above the Christian faith, as if from the situation alone. The only pertinent question is not whether pastors engage in the theological reinterpretation of the Christian faith, but simply whether they do so consciously and critically (rather than unconsciously and uncritically) and, hence, responsibly.

Witness and Theology: A Distinction

Let us begin our discussion of thinking theologically in the church with a simple distinction, one used by many theologians. (Of the many theologians whose work has most contributed to what follows, the more recent among them are: Schubert Ogden, David Tracy, Edward Farley, William Placher, and Paul M. van Buren.) It is the distinction between the work of the church and the work of the theologian in the church. The work of the church is to *make* the Christian witness to the gospel of Jesus Christ; the work of the theologian is to *criticize* the way in which the church makes its witness of faith, to *think* about this witness. Karl Barth, for example, makes such a distinction when he differentiates between the church's *language* about God and the way the church *tests its use* of this language (Barth, 1). This distinction is, first, not a separation; we cannot make the witness of faith without thinking about what we are doing and we cannot think about it without also making it, even if we only make it indirectly. Second, this distinction is only a relative, not an absolute, distinction. We might equally well say that it is merely a matter of emphasis. The *emphasis* of the church is more on making the Christian witness than on thinking critically about it, that of the theologian more on thinking about it than on making it. Another way to make the same point is simply to say, since after all we are usually talking here about one and the same person doing these two things, that in *some* moments I am more intent on making the Christian witness than I am on thinking about it and in *other* moments I am more intent on thinking about it than on making it. These moments need be no more separate than are the moments when I am thinking about what I want to say in a sermon and the moments in which I am saying it.

Some Suggested Criteria

The words "criticize" and "criticism" are often misunderstood these days to be synonymous with "destroy" and "destruction." This is *not* the way in which we are talking here of critical thinking. To be critical is, in the most elementary sense, simply to think; thinking cannot be done un-critically. When we are being uncritical we may be free-associating, but we are not thinking. When we ask the simplest of questions, questions like "how do we know this to be true?" and "how does that work?" we are thinking critically. To think critically is to do one's thinking in the light of certain defined and clarified *criteria.* Here we suggest some criteria that, we hope, will help prompt pastors to engage in theological thinking as they go about their task of teaching the Christian faith.

At the beginning of this part of our discussion we said that whenever we encounter the biblical community of faith we always find it *reinter-preting* its faith. We never find Israel or the church simply wallowing in uninterpreted experience; there is no such thing as uninterpreted experi-ence: "If we desire a record of uninterpreted experience, we must ask a stone to record its autobiography" (Whitehead 1979, 15). Hence we al-ways find the community of faith inheriting and reinterpreting its tradi-tion. It is under no compunction to say the same thing it has said before. Sometimes its reinterpretations will straightforwardly deny what it had previously affirmed: "As I live, says the Lord GOD, this proverb shall no more be used by you in Israel" (Ezek. 18:3).

When we ask *how* Israel reinterpreted its faith, by what standards, we are led to Israel's hermeneutical principles, the axioms in the light of which it reinterpreted its tradition. These three axioms provide us a way of formulating a norm of appropriateness for use in our task of interpret-ing, that is, understanding, the Christian faith. (1) The Bible is a monotheizing (not simply a monotheistic) literature. In every new context the community finds itself regularly struggling "within and against poly-theistic contexts to affirm God's oneness" (Sanders 1984, 52). In other words, it reflects a broad *theocentric* hermeneutic, one expressed in two further hermeneutical axioms, (2) the prophetic and (3) the constitutive. The prophetic axiom stipulates that God is the God of *all.* The constitutive axiom stresses that God is the particular redeemer of Israel or the church. In other words, the prophetic axiom says: God loves *all,* therefore do justice to them and do not think too highly of yourselves, while the con-stitutive axiom states: God loves *you.* You are especially cherished by God. The constitutive axiom bespeaks *promise,* the prophetic *challenge* (Sanders 1984, 53). Each gives voice to the grace of God, grace extended freely to *all* God's beloved, on the one hand, and on the other *even* to us. If we ask why there are these two hermeneutical axioms, the answer is that some situations require the one, and some the other. In moments of crisis and desperation, under persecution and attack, the community was reminded of God's particular love for it. In other, more well-to-do moments, when the community prospered and relaxed and failed to carry out its task and do justice to all God's beloved, especially the poor and the outcast, it was reminded that God is the God of all, not just of this group: "I have other sheep, that are not of this fold" (John 10:16).

We can put these three hermeneutic emphases together into one statement of a norm of appropriateness for interpreting the Christian faith. The *theocentric* emphasis of the biblical hermeneutic reminds us that, whatever the theological topic with which we are dealing, ultimately it is God with whom we have to do. So, number one, we must do all our witnessing and theologizing "to the greater glory of God" *(ad maiorem Dei gloriam,* as the Latin formula has it). We are well advised to remember that this God to whose greater glory we do our theologizing is the God of Israel, the maker of heaven and earth and our redeemer. The primary assertion that the doctrine of the Trinity sought to deny was that the God whom we know in Jesus Christ is *another* deity than the One whom Jesus called "Abba." The constitutive axiom re-presents to us God's special love for us, for *each* of us in this community and for *this* community, while the prophetic recalls to us God's love for *all* of God's creatures as well as God's commandment that we do justice to all of them. The constitutive promise of God's love and the prophetic command that we love and do justice are wrapped up with the overall theocentric emphasis in this way: The gospel, the good news, is that God is the God of a singular promise and a singular command: the promise of God's love offered freely graciously, to each and all and the command that we are to love God *with* all our selves and to love (do justice to) our neighbor *as* ourselves.

This statement of the gospel, then, we take as the norm (the standard or criterion) of appropriateness in the light of which we should scrutinize all our interpretations of the Christian faith. The argument underlying this claim is fairly straightforward: It is appropriate to interpret the Bible in the way in which the Bible interpreted itself. We should always ask whether the way we want to make the Christian witness truly testifies to the gospel of Jesus Christ. The first question is whether this or that piece of Christian witness is *appropriate* to the gospel, whether it is truly Christian. We even have to ask whether, for example, this or that construal of the historical Jesus or of the meaning of a biblical text is appropriate to the gospel; hence we do not take these understandings (of the historical Jesus or the biblical text) as norms of appropriateness. Notice that this way of formulating the gospel (the gracious promise of the love of God offered freely to each and all and, therefore, the command of God that justice be done to each and all of those whom God loves) is not a circle with one center but an ellipse with two foci: God's radically free, empowering grace, and God's command of justice. When Christian witness forgets the first, it invariably falls into works-righteousness; when it ignores the second, it comes to grief in cheap grace. Notice, too, that the emphasis on God's radically free grace affirms the truth of the Reformation principles *sola gratia, sola fide,* by grace alone, by faith alone. Our justification is *by* God's grace, apprehended *through* our response of faith. At the same time, the emphasis on God's command that justice be done reminds us that our lives are to be radically transformed by God's liberating grace and put at the service of the neighbor.

The second and third criteria have to do with intelligibility, in two forms: theoretical and moral. Here it is important to observe that in being concerned with intelligibility we are not importing into the tradition something from outside it. A living tradition itself is always concerned with intelligibility, with "making sense" of the situation and of the inheritance of faith. The Bible itself is "the result of many efforts over some 1500 to 1800 years and through five different culture eras to monotheize over against a massive cultural backdrop of polytheism" (Sanders 1984, 43). That the scriptures themselves represent a process of reinterpretation through five major cultural epochs itself testifies to the fact that the biblical tradition persistently sought to "make sense" of itself in new situations as well as to make sense of new situations in the light of its legacy of faith.

Hence the witness of the church must be comprehensible. We must be able to understand it if it is to speak to us (although our understanding needs to be transformed by the Christian witness, the result is nevertheless a transformed understanding). Our witness must "make sense"; it must be comprehensible, coherent, and have illuminating power. What Paul refers to as the "truth of the gospel" (Gal. 2:5) is not something to which confusion and falsehood can bear witness. The gospel is God's liberating truth: "you will know the truth, and the truth will make you free" (John 8:32). Christian testimony to God's liberating truth must itself be true, worthy of being believed. We agree with Leith and others that intelligibility does not mean "proof." We take it to be a way of showing that the Christian faith is commendable. It is not enough merely to seek to be appropriate to the tradition and, in that sense, truthful, because the tradition drastically reinterpreted itself in striking and dramatic ways and frequently sought to understand its faith. The tradition itself commands us to stand ready "to make a defense *(apologian)* to any one who calls you to account *(logon)* for the hope that is in you" (1 Peter 3:15).

When we say that the gospel is the promise of the love of God graciously offered to each and all and the (dual) command of God that we love God with all ourselves and our neighbors as ourselves, we are not saying that, as Christians, this is to us merely a matter of taste. The gospel "insists on its universality, because it is either that or a passing fancy" (Whitehead 1926, 133). We are saying that as we see things this is the truth, the only way in which we can, in any ultimate sense, genuinely understand ourselves and the only way in which we think *anyone* could appropriately understand herself or himself. It is true that in a relative sense we may legitimately understand ourselves in myriad ways, in terms of gender, race, nationality, income level, social class, interest groups, and hobbies. But the ultimate truth about oneself is *not* that one is, say, an American or a coin collector. Instead, we think the only way in which I may truly understand myself in any ultimate sense is in terms of, and only in terms of, the love of God freely offered to me, which love in turn commands radical commitment to meet the needs of the neighbor as well as to love God. If we understand ourselves differently, in any ultimate sense, we simply misunderstand ourselves.

Christians claim, in other words, to have a grasp on truth, perhaps not *the* grasp on truth but certainly a grasp on truth. One danger churches face today is relativism, the fear that any claim to truth is both presumptuous and oppressive. The danger here is that our concern with openness and pluralism will lead us to lose any sense of being exposed to the truth in and through Christian faith and witness. The other danger is that of idolatry, confusing our grasp on truth with truth itself, regarding our interpretation of matters of ultimacy as itself ultimate. Since Christians regard what truth they have as a gift from God, we should remember to speak humbly and gratefully of what has been given us to know.

Whitehead once remarked of what he called "rational religion," that it "appeals to the direct intuition of special occasions, and to the elucidatory power of its concepts for all occasions" (Whitehead 1926, 31). Such a religion, he said, is one "whose beliefs and rituals have been reorganized with the aim of making it the central element in a coherent ordering of life—an ordering which shall be coherent both in respect to the elucidation of thought, and in respect to the direction of conduct towards a unified purpose commanding ethical approval" (Whitehead 1926, 30). Here we have the claim that religion at its best functions to provide a way to "make sense" of life with regard both to how we *understand* things and to how we *conduct ourselves* morally, that is, both theoretically and practically.

H. Richard Niebuhr quoted and paraphrased Whitehead's definition of "rational religion" to provide the most influential definition of revelation offered by an American theologian:

> The special occasion to which we appeal in the Christian church is called Jesus Christ, in whom we see the righteousness of God, his power and wisdom. But from that special occasion we also derive the concepts which make possible the elucidation of all the events in our history. *Revelation means this intelligible event which makes all other events intelligible. . . . Revelation means the point at which we can begin to think and act as members of an intelligible and intelligent world of persons* (Niebuhr, 93, 94; emphasis ours).

There are two ways to make the point here, one simple and direct, the other more complicated. The simple and direct route is to say that the gospel, our norm of appropriateness, itself requires both that we try to make sense of the Christian faith in ever-changing contexts (because it claims to be true and we must take responsibility for this truth) and that we seek to make the Christian witness in a morally credible way (because it commands us to do justice to the neighbor). In other words, the gospel, the norm of appropriateness itself, both gives and demands the possibility that we make sense of life in terms of it and that we struggle with figuring out what it means to live in the light of it.

The slightly more complicated way of making the same point occurs when we have recourse to the writings of the cultural anthropologist Clifford Geertz. Geertz views religion as "a semiotic concept of culture," by which he means that a religion is a symbol system or form of culture by means of which people communicate, perpetuate, and develop their knowledge about and attitudes toward life. Human beings, says Geertz, are "symbolizing, conceptualizing, meaning-seeking" animals whose "drive to make sense of experience, to give it form and order, is evidently as real and as pressing as the more familiar biological needs" (Geertz, 140ff.).

Religion, therefore, is a specific kind of synthesis or "fusion," having two aspects to which Geertz refers as "ethos" and "worldview." It is never merely worldview or metaphysics because "the holy bears within it everywhere a sense of intrinsic obligation: It not only encourages devotion, it demands it; it not only induces intellectual assent, it enforces emotional commitment" (Geertz, 126). Nor is religion ever merely ethics, because "the source of its emotional vitality is conceived to lie in the fidelity with which it expresses the fundamental nature of reality. The powerfully coercive 'ought' is felt to grow out of a comprehensive factual 'is,' and in such a way religion grounds the most specific requirements of human action in the most general contexts of human existence" (Geertz, 126).

Whitehead and Niebuhr, in short, were on target in commenting that Christian tradition, in interpreting the paradigmatic event that is at its heart, provides people with a way of thinking and acting intelligibly, with a way of being both intellectually and morally credible. That is, the Christian faith has two sides to it: an ethical, normative side that reflects "the underlying attitude toward themselves and their world" found in the life of the community, and a metaphysical side that embodies elements expressed in the community's "picture of the way things in sheer actuality are, their concept of nature, of self, of society" (Geertz, 126). Because the two are fused, the way of life is justified, made "intellectually reasonable by being shown to represent a way of life implied by the actual state of affairs which the world view describes, and the world view is made emotionally acceptable by being presented as an image of an actual state of affairs of which such a way of life is an authentic expression" (Geertz, 126).

Finally: The Nuts and Bolts

What we have been saying, then, is that those who would think theologically about how the church makes the Christian witness need to look over that witness (for example, the point of the sermon one plans to preach next week) and ask of it three questions: Is this point or this interpretation of the Christian faith (a) appropriate to the Christian message, (b) credible, and (c) morally plausible? We learn to *do* theology, finally, the way we learn to do anything else: by doing it. Here, as in basketball, practice makes perfect or, if not perfect, at least better. It is by persistently asking these questions (not by reciting old, tired answers to them) both of the tradition and of one's own most cherished theological views that we eventually get the hang of doing theology. We must also, of course, keep asking ourselves whether we are satisfied with our own understandings of what counts for appropriateness, credibility, and moral plausibility. That sounds endless, you might say. It is. It is also inescapable if we are responsible to our commitments to be ministers of word and sacrament, teachers of the Christian faith.

These three concerns are by no means separate from one another; they are three aspects of one complex critical principle. The Christian message itself requires of us intellectual and moral accountability (love God with all your mind and your neighbor as yourself); not to be so accountable is not only to fail to make sense or to fail to be morally believable, it is also to be inappropriate to the tradition itself.

To take the nuts-and-bolts approach to doing theology, hence, is simply to require oneself to ask, week by week, whether and how one's understanding of the point of a prospective sermon or church school lesson or funeral homily or whatever is appropriate to the gospel, and is it intellectually and morally credible. Recalling our earlier discussion of the Reformers' preference for a pluralistic and collegial approach to teaching authority in the church, we must add that it is wise to ask these questions in the company of a diverse group of committed Christians—women, men, laity, clergy, African-Americans, whites, and others. Learning to ask such questions of the tradition and of oneself, patiently pursuing them, we come to see that if the revelation of God in Jesus Christ *really* is revelation, then, as Niebuhr said, it does make sense of all the other events in our history. All of this is a heady and exciting journey. We discover that "the neighbor" whom we are to love is a much more expansive concept than we had ever thought; that this concept includes the "stranger" whom we are to love as we love ourselves and all kinds of other people and creatures, perhaps the biosphere itself. The quest for theological understanding is nothing less than an incredible journey of spiritual growth, a growth that, by God's grace, *can* enable us to live transformed lives of greater devotion, greater freedom, and greater relatedness to all the wide diversity of our human neighbors and the rest of the created order as well. It is a journey that can only be traversed doggedly, or faithfully one might say, one step at a time, steadfastly criticizing one's own past understandings. That's the nuts and bolts of it.

5
THE SERMON AS
TEACHING EVENT
TODAY

In earlier chapters, we noted conditions in the church and world of today that call for a renewal of the teaching sermon. We traced teaching as a leading motif in the preaching of Judaism and Christianity. In this chapter, we turn to a constructive proposal for understanding the sermon as a teaching event, and we offer selected models for the teaching sermon.

The Teaching Sermon in Broad Perspective

Recent homiletics textbooks tend to view the teaching sermon as a specialized type of preaching, sometimes equating the teaching sermon with the doctrinal sermon. In this view, the purpose of the doctrinal sermon is to inform the congregation concerning some aspect of Christian doctrine. For instance, a teaching sermon on the Christian understanding of prayer might define prayer, develop an argument for the importance of prayer, and provide instruction in the act of praying. While the doctrinal sermon (so understood) might make use of scripture, the primary purpose of such a sermon is not biblical exposition but interpretation of doctrine. Of course, every sermon is preached through the lens of Christian doctrine (whether the preacher is conscious of it or not!) but the primary focus of the doctrinal sermon is to explain basic Christian beliefs.

To be sure, the contemporary pulpit has an important place for such preaching. But it is much too restrictive to equate the doctrinal sermon with the teaching sermon. For in addition to instruction in Christian doctrine per se, the congregation needs instruction in the content of the Bible (and in how to interpret the Bible), on the meaning of personal and social experience in the light of the gospel, as well as on appropriate moral beliefs and behavior.

Some authors in contemporary homiletics regard the teaching sermon as one that communicates ideas, makes points, or exchanges information (Blackwood, 141; Jensen, 11). The subject matter of the teaching sermon may be a biblical text, a Christian doctrine, or some aspect of contemporary experience. Richard Jensen uses a teaching sermon based on a passage from the Bible as a way of illustrating the traits of the teaching sermon generally. Its goal is to "teach the lessons of the text." These lessons are often "abstracted from the text." The sermon itself is directed to the mind of the listener and the sermon is developed in a "logical sequential and linear manner." The sermon is prepared following the rules for the preparation of written material (Jensen, 27ff.).

This understanding of the teaching sermon reduces the act of teaching to the transmission of information according to a single formula without regard for subject matter or situation. While such a conception of the teaching sermon has something to commend it, it goes awry at two points. For one, teaching today is much more broadly conceived as an act in which the teacher helps people to learn to see (and to be) in the world in ways appropriate to the normative vision of the community. For another, while teaching may involve the exchange of information, it may also draw upon any number of pedagogical approaches, ranging from Socratic dialogue to the telling of parables that are designed to cause the hearer to think afresh concerning the relationship of the self, the world, and the normative vision of the community. Maria Harris, in fact, shows that the Christian teacher draws upon the deepest powers of the religious imagination (Harris, 2–22).

In the tradition of the preaching of Israel and of the church (especially the tradition of the Reformation), we propose that today's preacher view every sermon to an established congregation as a teaching event. This requires that we come to a clear understanding of teaching and of the teaching sermon.

As a corollary, we agree with David Buttrick that the church today needs to give renewed attention to evangelistic witness (Buttrick, 226–227; see also Craddock 1978, 108). The teaching sermon as conceived here is addressed primarily to an established Christian community and to those who are considering identifying with such a community. The purpose of the teaching sermon is to build up the congregation in faith.

Buttrick refers to evangelistic witness as "out-church preaching" because it takes place outside settled congregations and is ideally carried out by the laity (Buttrick, 226). The forms of evangelistic witness can be quite varied and can involve both actions and words. Buttrick correctly urges

that when evangelistic witness takes the form of action, it should be accompanied by an interpretive statement that connects the act of witness to
the gospel.

However, contemporary Christians need instruction in bearing spoken
witness in the world. As Buttrick notes, "The message that many lay
people hand out is a vapid, semi-sincere sales pitch for local parish programs: 'Come to our church. We have a keen pastor, a men's bowling
league, P.E.T. classes, a counseling center, the biggest Youth Club in town
and, oh yes, if you like to sing, our music program with a bell choir is
super. We're a full-service church' " (Buttrick, 226). Beyond the sales
pitch, the laity need to be able to "give an account of the hope" that is in
them. The teaching sermon is one way by which the congregation can
learn how to conceive and give such an account.

Before discussing the characteristics of the teaching sermon, we pause
to consider what may be one of the most important steps on the journey
to preparing the teaching sermon: the self-conscious decision to preach in
a teaching mode. This may be a new perspective for pastors who habitually think of preaching in other terms. For instance, some primarily think
of preaching as an instrument for the purpose of conversion or as counseling on a mass scale or for the purpose of maintaining the institutional
health of the local congregation (for example, raising the budget or re-
cruiting youth-group sponsors) or as lobbying for a particular social
agenda. To think of the sermon as an act of teaching may require a shift of
gears. Instead of beginning with a question such as "With what personal
need am I going to help the congregation this week?" or "What political
action am I going to urge the congregation to take this week," the leading
question may be, "What do we need to learn as a community this week
and in these upcoming weeks?" The latter question provides a distinctive
angle of vision from which to go about sermon preparation.

Characteristics of the
Teaching Sermon

The teaching sermon helps the congregation name the world (and the
congregation's experience in the world) in the terms of the gospel. As
noted earlier, we understand the gospel to be the news that God loves
each and every created thing and that this love calls for justice for each
and every created thing.

Following the lead of Deuteronomy and in the tradition of both Judaism and the church, we may say that teaching involves two significant
moments. The first is enabling the community to recall (or to learn) the

content of the gospel as well as the traditions of our faith from the time of the Bible to the present day. The other is the interpretation of the gospel (and the tradition) for the sake of the living community. We have earlier called this process "traditioning."

Charles Blaisdell perceptively points out that this naming of the world often involves two things. First, the teaching preacher must often expose the fact that the congregation typically views the world (and its life therein) in purely human terms and without reference to the transcendent God. Second, the preacher moves beyond exposé to name the world in the terms of the gospel. Thus, "the minister-as-teacher in his or her interaction with the world creates, as it were, a different world. Or, alternatively put, the minister-as-teacher, given his or her rootedness in the transcendent, discloses what the world is like when it is informed and structured by the transcendent" (Blaisdell, 49). Such "veracious preaching constructs or discerns an alternative to the idolatries present before the preacher" (Blaisdell, 52). Blaisdell points out that the "teacher-preacher can fail at his or her task when what is spoken is neither 'good' nor 'news.' If preaching cannot name an alternative to the claimed ultimacy of the purely human, then it is not news; if it presents its news with a tacit admission that the news really cannot change us, then it is not good" (Blaisdell, 52).

Thus, in the language of the sociology of knowledge, the preacher offers the congregation a symbolic universe that is defined by the gospel (Berger and Luckmann, 85–118). The preacher helps the congregation "tag" aspects of the world with names that help the congregation to recognize God's presence and purpose as well as to know how to respond appropriately to that presence and purpose. For instance, the sermon can identify sin and its manifestations in the world; the sermon can name the gospel and show the significance of the gospel for a world caught in the grip of sin; the sermon can outline behavior and values that are consistent with the gospel. The sermon thus deals with two of the great questions of life: Who are we? What are we to do?

One of the writers of this book has a daughter named Genesis. When Genesis was about three years old, she was in worship with her parents. The pastor was preaching on a text from the first book of the Bible. The sermon began with a story from modern life; our daughter was sitting beside us in the pew, quietly looking at a child's book. The pastor then shifted the sermon directly to the passage from scripture. The first time he spoke the name of the book, "Genesis," our daughter lifted her face from the child's book with a look of recognition and expectation. The preacher called her by name. She responded with trust and hope. And that moment pictures a primary purpose of Christian preaching.

As we noted earlier, teaching employs the highest and most imaginative powers of the teacher. The teacher seeks to create the best possible environment in which the learner can receive the material being taught and can make a responsible choice of whether to accept or to reject (or to make another response to) the material. Because teaching is a creative act, there is no single formula for the teaching sermon. However, although quite diverse in form, teaching sermons manifest similar characteristics. We outline fifteen characteristics of the teaching sermon.

1. *The teaching sermon helps the listeners remember—or learn—the content of the gospel.* It often helps the listeners become acquainted with the major witnesses to the gospel in the history of Israel and the church. Through the teaching sermon, the listener will typically become acquainted with a piece of the tradition not known before or will become reacquainted with a piece of the tradition once known but now forgotten or will review a familiar piece of the tradition in a new way.

Aiden Kavanaugh points out that, at times, the preacher may not so much "instruct the unknowing in the Unknown," as she or he may "trigger the myriad awarenesses of that same absolute reality all members of the group bring with them" (Kavanaugh, 43). In the same way, Thomas G. Long notes that "we who preach do not have the whole gospel in our grasp ready to drop it into empty vessels. Our task is not simply to proclaim the gospel *to* them, but to recognize it *in* them as well, to name it, celebrate it, nurture and guide it" (Long 1988, 62).

To put the matter simply, we cannot draw upon and interpret a tradition that we do not know. Developing familiarity with the gospel, with the historic witnesses to the gospel, and with the occurrences of the gospel in our own setting is a first important step.

2. *The teaching sermon helps the listeners reflect critically on the situation of the community.* If the purpose of the teaching sermon is to help us name *the world* in the terms of the gospel, then it follows that we must know the world so that we will name the world as it is and will not misname it or name it in caricature. Thus, the teaching sermon will help us clarify the cultural, psychological, economic, political, religious, cosmological factors that are pertinent to the sermon at hand. However, it is not enough for these things simply to be described phenomenologically in a Christian sermon. "No, if we address situations, somewhere, somehow, there must be a contending with our assumptions as well as a rereading of situations in the light of revelation" (Buttrick, 417). The teaching sermon will help

us assess the adequacy of our view of the world in the light of the gospel and its norms.

3. *The teaching sermon helps the listeners interpret the significance of the gospel (and the tradition) for the contemporary community.* When the sermon draws only upon the gospel (the promise of God's love for each and all and the command for justice for each and all) as its theological center, the preacher's job is relatively straightforward. The preacher conducts an exegesis of the situation of the community in order to determine whether the community has a greater need to hear the word of promise or the word of command. For instance, if the church is losing confidence in God's presence, the community likely needs the assurance of God's promise. If the community is endorsing values and practices that devalue others, then the community likely needs to hear the call for justice for each and all.

Of course, the themes of love and justice are so closely intertwined that the preacher will nearly always consider both in a single sermon. The reminder of God's universal love necessarily calls forth the recognition that God's love is for all. But in a given sermon, emphasis will often be more on one pole of the gospel than on the other.

The preacher's task is more complicated when the preacher brings a piece of the tradition (such as a biblical text) into the sermon. In this case, the preacher encounters the hermeneutical problem. The hermeneutical problem arises from the recognition that the worldview (including theological assumptions) of the text is different from the worldview of the contemporary community. This raises the question of what the text means (or does not mean) for the current church.

One of the simplest examples of the hermeneutical problem is the phenomenon of idolatry. At various moments in the world of the Bible, people worshiped false gods (represented in the world by idols). The Bible frequently chides the people to avoid idolatry. Yet, in late twentieth-century North America, few people actually worship (in the liturgical sense) idols. Hence, the question is raised, What does a passage such as the following have to say to us? "Do not turn to idols or make for yourselves molten gods" (Lev. 19:4a).

Slavery provides another example. From Genesis to Revelation, the Bible generally presumes the validity of slavery as a social institution. What is today's community to make of a text such as 1 Peter 2:18–19? "Servants, be submissive to your masters with all respect, not only to the kind and gentle but also to the overbearing. For one is approved if, mindful of God, he endures pain while suffering unjustly."

The preacher cannot mechanically reproduce the tradition (copy-machine fashion) but must consider the witness of the tradition and what that witness might—and might not—have to say to our generation. In this respect, it is helpful to remember that the preacher's call is not to "preach the Bible" but to preach the gospel. Each piece of the tradition makes a witness concerning the nature of God, God's relationship with the world, and the human response to God. Sometimes this witness is a helpful corrective to contemporary faith, but sometimes the witness of the historical tradition (including the Bible) undercuts the gospel, human sensibility, or moral behavior. Thus, the teaching preacher must converse with the tradition in order to determine what the tradition has to say to the living body.

This conversation typically moves in three stages. First, through hardnosed exegesis, the teacher determines the witness of the text. The preacher's exegesis may confirm our preunderstanding of the text or it may conclude that we have misunderstood the witness of the text and that we need to adopt a radically revised understanding of the text.

Second, the preacher assesses the text in the light of the norms of appropriateness, intelligibility, and moral credibility. At the same time, the preacher thinks of her or his understanding of the gospel and the world in the light of the witness of the text. The preacher may find that the text accurately names his or her experience or that the text calls for the preacher to enlarge (or rethink) some aspect of the gospel.

Third, the preacher clearly establishes her or his hermeneutical relationship with the text. The preacher has four possible hermeneutical relationships with the text. (a) When the text is appropriate, intelligible, and moral, the preacher can preach the gospel through the witness of the text. (b) When the text presents some difficulties but is not at heart inappropriate or immoral, the preacher may partially agree with the text and partially disagree. For example, the text may make a witness concerning God's nature and love that is quite appropriate, but the text may presume a cosmology that we no longer share. The preacher would then show points at which the text is instructive and points at which the text is no longer helpful and would help us see what sense we can make of difficulties. (c) When the text is inappropriate to the gospel, unintelligible, or morally offensive, the minister will preach against the text. The preacher states plainly that the text is no longer instructive or authoritative for the church and shows why. (d) The preacher can ignore a text. This is especially attractive when the text poses difficulties for today's listener. But to ignore a text is to miss a teaching moment and can leave the impression that the community endorses the viewpoint of the text.

4. *The content of the teaching sermon is appropriate to the gospel.* The

positions advocated in the homily will be consistent with the conviction
that God loves each and all.

5. *The content of the teaching sermon is intelligible.* As noted earlier in
the volume, Christian teaching concerning God, God's activity in the
world, and the possibilities of the world will be consistent with the ways
in'which we think about the world today. Christian preaching will un-
pack the inner logic of the Christian faith and will show how the Christian faith is a coherent and sensible way of viewing the world today.
Furthermore, the methods of development and argument in the sermon
should be open to the examination of the listeners.

6. *The content of the teaching sermon is morally credible.* The theses of the
sermon assume that all human beings as well as the natural realm are to
be treated in ways that assert that each and every created being is loved
unconditionally by God. The sermon will never degrade another person
or license the abuse of the natural world. In the course of telling the truth,
the viewpoints, values, and practices of others will often be critiqued by
the preacher. But such criticism will always occur in the context of the
preacher's acknowledgment of the love of God for the other and God's
call for justice for the other.

7. *The teaching sermon teaches both in its content and by its methodology.*
To be sure, the sermon always teaches the content of the gospel. At the
same time, the teaching sermon offers the listeners a clear model of how
to think theologically about the significance of the Christian tradition for
the world today. The ways in which the preacher reasons in the course of
the sermon teach the people how to reason as they come to judgments
concerning faith and its relationship to life.

8. *The teaching sermon has a clear purpose.* For instance, the preacher
may want the congregation to learn the meaning of the gospel, to experience the grace of God through the medium of the sermon, and, hence, to
become gracious in their view and treatment of others.

9. *The teaching sermon employs a communication strategy that is appropriate to the purpose of the sermon.* For example, a sermon whose purpose is
basically informational may call upon the preacher to think of how creatively to convey information so that the information will have a good
chance of being remembered. If the sermon needs to deconstruct a part of
the worldview of the hearers, the preacher may want to create a parable
that causes the listeners to look at their world from a new perspective. In
any case, the teaching preacher will need to be aware of the worldview(s)
of those who hear the sermon in order to conceive a homiletical strategy
that will stand a good chance of getting a fair hearing.

10. The teaching sermon is delivered in a way that is appropriate to the gospel. The whole of the preaching event teaches, so the preacher will want to speak and act in the pulpit in ways that embody God's love for the world and in ways that teach that God is alive and passionate. Thus, the preacher will want to be authentic and lively. And the style of the delivery should be consonant with the tone of the sermon. A passage on sadness would be delivered in a sober mood while a passage on joy would be delivered joyfully. In a sermon on love, the delivery undercuts the content when the preacher speaks in harsh, angry tones and bangs his or her fist on the pulpit.

11. The teaching preacher respects the freedom of the listeners to say no to the sermon. This is more than the practical recognition that some people will disagree with the preacher. To respect the right of the people to disagree is to take them seriously precisely because the subject matter under discussion is serious. Indeed, the preacher and the people are discussing what is true and what is not. Because the stakes are high, the preacher seeks for all to bring their best powers of analysis and reasoning to the sermon.

12. A teaching minister learns from others. Teaching ministers are especially willing to learn from those who understand the world from standpoints that are not immediately available to the minister, for example, artists, psychologists, sociologists, economists, political analysts, physical scientists, persons of different racial and ethnic backgrounds. Ministers may even be surprised at what they learn from sensitive members of the congregation who have no credentials that would suggest that these persons have insight to offer to the ministers beyond their own reflection on life experience. From this vantage point, one of the best preparations for the work of preaching is simply to live and to reflect on what happens in life.

13. In the teaching sermon, the preacher draws upon the best of what we know regarding how people learn. The chief tenets of our awareness follow.

> In the optimum learning environment, the teacher and the students are bonded together in a relationship of trust and mutual support. In particular, the teacher affirms the worth of the learners as persons, and the teacher makes herself or himself available to the students (Roberts, 12). Thus, a foundation of the teaching sermon is a strong, trusted pastoral relationship between the pastoral teacher and the congregation.
>
> Within this environment, the teacher encourages the learners to take

risks in trying new ways of thinking and shows support and encourage-
ment even when the learners seem to fail. As D. Bruce Roberts notes, "It
is clear that cutting, sarcastic or combative styles of behavior in the
classroom will not support or sustain the student through the experience
of risk in learning to think critically" (Roberts, 14). The same is true in
the arena of preaching.

As a corollary, the teacher often introduces (into the teaching situation) factors that produce dissonance in the mind of the listener. The
dissonance may be as small as getting the learners to recognize that they
do not possess knowledge that could prove helpful to them, or it may be
as serious as the preacher helping the listeners to recognize basic con-
flicts between the values of the gospel and the everyday values of the
listeners. The contradiction thus experienced "facilitates growth precisely because it creates doubt and intensifies the search for more adequate views of understanding" (Roberts, 14–15). Thus, dissonance helps
open the listeners to entertaining new perspectives.

The teacher helps the students integrate the new perspectives that
come from individual learnings into the larger patterns of students'
thinking and acting. A sermon on the importance of forgiving one another, for instance, should ultimately be connected to God's forgiveness
of the human race and to the nature of God.

When a preacher develops an idea or concept in the course of a sermon, the preacher needs to use an image that will give the listeners a
picture of the concept (Buttrick, 32).

The self-conscious use of learning theory in the development and presentation of sermons cannot guarantee learning on the parts of the congregants, but it can help create an environment that is learner-friendly.

14. *Each teaching sermon will be informed by a comprehensive vision of God
and God's relationship with the world* such that each sermon is coherent with
the overall theological clarity of the preacher. All the sermons from the
same preacher will articulate a consistent viewpoint. The preacher teaches
only one thing: the gospel. But from time to time the preacher looks at the
gospel and its relationship to the congregation through different windows.
One week, the window may be a text from the book of Joshua. Another
week the window may be the Christian doctrine of baptism. Still another week, the window may be the Christian interpretation of natural
disaster, such as an earthquake. But, regardless of the subject matter for
the particular week, the sermon is refracted through the lens of a well-
defined grasp of the gospel.

15. *The teaching sermon helps the community discern the implications of the gospel (as presented through the sermon) for life.* One reason that many of us have difficulty remembering the details of subjects we studied in high school or college is that many of the details of the subjects were given to us with no attention to their relationship to our ongoing experience. We tend to take to heart those things that relate directly to us. Thus, the preacher will want to give some direct points at which the sermon illuminates the lives of the listeners and points at which the life experience of the listeners illuminates the tradition.

Thus, the teaching sermon does not so much announce the news of the gospel (as if for the first time) as much as it helps the congregation grasp the import of the gospel for its life and for the life of the cosmos.

Preachers often lament the inability of the congregation to recall the contents of particular sermons. This situation will likely not be alleviated by a purposeful shift to preaching from a teaching perspective. However, the fact that parishioners cannot regurgitate the contents of a specific sermon need not worry the preacher as long as parishioners are growing in their vision and trust of God and in their capacity to witness to the gospel. Individual sermons contribute in an incremental way to the development of the listeners' theological vision, method, and capacity for witness. By analogy, as a child, this writer was not a good student in arithmetic. I cannot, in fact, remember a single lesson in arithmetic. But today, I can add, subtract, multiply, and divide. In this spirit, Thomas Long adds that "a preacher may well have reason to rejoice over a hearer who cannot recall what was said but who is still savoring the places in her life where the sermon made an impact, the places where she attached pieces of her own experience to a sermonic pattern she can no longer see" (Long 1988, 60).

Some Forms for the
Teaching Sermon

The question naturally arises, When the basic direction of the content of the sermon is in hand, how do I put together a teaching sermon? We now describe briefly several possibilities for conceiving and outlining sermons that have a teaching quality. We do not give an exhaustive catalog but mention only several sermon forms that may stimulate the preacher's thinking about practical matters in developing teaching sermons. Most of these models presuppose the use of a biblical text as a starting point but could be adapted to topical preaching. Some of these models overlap in one way or another.

1. The simple form of exegesis, exposition, application. This is perhaps the simplest form for the teaching sermon. One can almost think of
it as a container into which to pour thought. The form consists of five
easily defined parts. The parts, their function, and their approximate percentage contribution to the length of the sermon follow.

> *Introduction* (5–15 percent). The introduction reveals the subject mat-
> ter of the sermon and helps the listeners see that the subject matter is
> important to them.
> *Exegesis* (25 percent). The exegesis establishes the witness of the text
> in the light of its historical and literary contexts.
> *Theological Analysis* (25 percent). In theological analysis, the preacher
> evaluates the witness of the text according to the norms of appropriate-
> ness to the gospel, intelligibility, and moral credibility. The analysis shows
> whether we agree with the text, partially agree (and partially disagree), or
> plainly disagree.
> *Application* (25 percent). The application states clearly "what we
> learn" from the witness of the text. The preacher helps the people apply
> the text to their concrete situation.
> *Conclusion* (5–15 percent). The conclusion draws the sermon to an
> appropriate end. It may do so by telling a story that embodies the main
> lesson of the sermon, by summarizing the argument of the sermon, by
> raising questions for further consideration on the part of the listeners, or
> in some other manner that seems a fitting end for the particular sermon.

The obvious advantages of this form are ease of preparation for the pastor
and clarity of thought for both pastor and parishioners. The major disad-
vantage is that the form can become quite wooden and lifeless. When
used every week, it can become anesthetic.

2. A conversational model. Conversation is currently and widely
viewed as a model for theological discourse. David Tracy describes conversation as an occasion wherein "we learn to give in to the movement
required by questions worth exploring." Indeed, "the movement in conversation is questioning itself. Neither my present opinions on the question nor the text's original response to the question but the question itself
must control every conversation. A conversation is a rare phenomenon,
even for Socrates. It is not a confrontation. It is not a debate. It is not an
exam. It is questioning itself. It is a willingness to follow the question
wherever it may go. It is dia-logue" (Tracy 1987, 18).

Conversation contains many forms of content, such as questions, arguments, stories, expostulations, propositions (sometimes tentatively tested), statements of hopes and fears. Whatever the form of conversation, Tracy notes that conversations follow hard rules. "Say only what you mean; say it as accurately as you can; listen to and respect what the other says, however different the other; be willing to correct or defend your opinions if challenged by other conversation partners; be willing to argue, if necessary, to confront if demanded, to endure necessary conflict, but change your mind if the evidence suggests it" (Tracy 1987, 19).

We usually think of a conversation as taking place when two or more people let their talk be governed by the exploration of the controlling questions. But we can also enter into conversation with texts. Indeed, we respond to texts much as we respond to living conversation partners. "We inquire. We question. We converse. Just as there is no purely autonomous text, so too there is no purely passive reader. There is only that interaction named conversation" (Tracy 1987, 19).

When preaching from a biblical text (or some other piece of tradition), the preacher carries on a conversation with the congregation concerning issues raised by the text. Long ago, Reuel Howe noted that preaching can be monological in method but dialogical in principle. Preaching takes on a conversational character when "the speaker feels responsible for and responds to the patterns of experience and understanding" which the listeners bring to the situation so that the listeners are encouraged to wrestle with their own meanings in relationship to the preacher's meaning (Howe, 47).

This suggests that the sermon might be developed after the pattern of conversation. David Buttrick has recently proposed that sermons can be structured according to the pattern of "conversational association." Instead of conceiving of the sermon as a series of themes that hang on an outline rather like sheets hanging on a clothesline, Buttrick thinks of the sermon as a series of "moves" that travel in the sermon in the same way that ideas and images unfold in the course of conversation (Buttrick, 71). In conversation, one idea or question leads naturally to another. The logic of conversations appears in such things as the connective words (for example, "but," "and," "yet," "so") and in shifts of perspective as from the past to the present or from narrow focus to wider focus (Buttrick, 71–72).

The sermon comprises a series of four to six moves. The move is the basic unit of the sermon and is about three or four minutes in length. Buttrick's detailed wisdom on the development of moves can be found in his massive *Homiletic* (23–28). For our purpose now, it is enough to note that each move is a module of thought that functions like a short section of a conversation. The sermon joins the moves together so that the mind of the listener travels with the preacher from one association to another even as conversation partners travel from one topic to another.

We might think of a sermon in a simple structure such as the following.

Move one:	A beginning that focuses the subject of the sermon.
Move two:	"And so we usually think . . . "
Move three:	"But there are some factors that interfere with this way of thinking . . . "
Move four:	"These very obstacles cause us to look again at the tradition and to discover that we have overlooked some very important details . . . "
Move five:	A conclusion that seeks for the effect of the gospel to continue in the consciousness of the hearer.

The questions that are raised by a text or subject sometimes offer a natural pattern by which to organize the sermon.

3. The sermon as a form of contemporary midrash. The Hebrew word "midrash" essentially means "interpretation." It is typically used by current biblical scholars to refer to Jewish modes of interpreting the sacred scriptures of Judaism in the Hellenistic era (c. 300 B.C.E. to 200 C.E.), but it can be used more generally. The underlying principle of the many forms of midrash is that the ancient text can prove illuminating to the contemporary community if the text is interpreted carefully. In its highest moments, midrash itself (the act of interpretation) was considered a part of the process of revelation.

There were many types of midrashic exposition of sacred texts (see Neusner 1983; Neusner 1987; Neusner 1989). We call attention to one form of midrash that offers a model for the contemporary sermon: that mode of interpretation which gives a unit-by-unit exposition of the meaning of a passage (Neusner 1989, 59–97). The exposition sometimes proceeds word by word, sometimes phrase by phrase, sometimes sentence by sentence. But in all cases, the interpretation is controlled by a careful and close reading of the text itself and by the best principles of rabbinic exegesis.

A caveat: the rabbis who produced the midrashic texts of antiquity sometimes followed rules of interpretation that today's critically trained preacher can no longer embrace. Furthermore, the critically informed preacher of today may be reluctant to embrace this approach because of its extensive use by preachers of radically differing theological persuasion who appear on television while brandishing limp-backed Bibles as they make their fiery way word by word through texts. Some of these latter preachers employ hermeneutical methods that cannot be considered appropriate to the gospel, intelligible, or moral.

However, the method of interpreting a text unit by unit can make full use of the best historical-critical and literary-critical biblical scholarship. And the midrashic approach (as we have designated it here) can be fully informed by an appropriate, intelligible, and morally credible theology.

If the preacher elects to preach in this fashion, it will be important to encourage church members to bring their Bibles to worship so they can follow the exposition carefully.

The advantages of such an approach are clear. It helps the congregation to pay close attention to the text itself. (Indeed, the Bible is sometimes better—or at least more interesting—than its interpreters!) Exposure to the text may bring significant theological issues into the minds of the listeners. By moving systematically through a text, the preacher has a wonderful opportunity to acquaint the congregation with historical, literary, and cultural allusions that clarify the meaning of the text. Such an approach can thus help overcome the biblical illiteracy that plagues our churches. The method also provides a model for the reading and general use of the Bible by laypeople. By observing the kinds of questions that the pastor raises and by observing how the pastor deals with those questions, the laypeople are prepared to engage in such explorations themselves. Furthermore, the outline of the text sometimes provides a natural outline by which to follow the interpretation of the text. And if the pastor is preaching against the text, the congregation will have a clear idea of what is being preached against and why. This approach lends itself especially well to preaching through books of the Bible or large sections within specific books.

This approach also has potential difficulties. It can be incredibly boring if the preacher is not lively and imaginative in presenting the interpretation of the text. By concentrating on the details of the text, it is easy to lose sight of the big picture. One can easily slip into thinking that giving an exegesis of the historical or literary meaning of the text is the same as showing the contemporary theological significance. And the approach can subtly contribute to bibliolatry.

Four keys can help contribute to the success of the program of preaching in this fashion. One is to help the congregation become conscious that the text is interpreted through the lens of a cogent theological position. Another key is for the preacher to be selective in the details that she considers in the course of interpretation. Still another key is to communicate the *major* claims of the text so that the sermon has a driving thrust. Finally, the preacher must show the pertinence of the text as a lens through which to cast the light of the gospel on the congregation.

In the case of texts with which the preacher is in agreement, the use of the hermeneutic of analogy is often very helpful. If the text is from 1 Corinthians, the preacher might ask, How are we today similar to (analogous to) the Corinthian Christians to whom the passage is addressed?

4. The simple topical sermon. From time to time the preacher may find it important to preach on a subject that arises from outside the Bible and (or) upon which the Bible has precious little to say. For instance, the Bible gives us no direct interpretation of the phenomenon of AIDS. Or the preacher may wish to preach on a Christian doctrine as such. Baptism, for instance, is a subject on which the current church desperately needs instruction. However, the earliest Christian literature contains dozens of images of baptism. Thus, one cannot simply preach on "the" biblical meaning of baptism. The preacher is better served to preach on the topic of baptism, bringing into the sermon appropriate references to the Bible, the tradition, the denomination's statements on the meaning of baptism, our experience. (For more detailed discussion of sermons of this type, see Buttrick, 427–448.)

A simple approach to the topical sermon is inspired by the first model mentioned above.

Introduction (5–15 percent). The introduction introduces the topic and suggests that the topic is of importance to the congregation.

Description of the Topic (25 percent). The preacher describes the topic. How do we encounter it? How do we perceive it? If the subject is a personal or social phenomenon, the preacher will want to provide accurate information. If the subject is a Christian doctrine, the preacher will likewise wish to describe the doctrine with precision.

Theological Analysis of the Topic (25 percent). In theological analysis, the preacher evaluates the topic in the light of the norms of appropriateness to the gospel, intelligibility, and moral credibility.

Implications (25 percent). The preacher draws out the implications of the Christian evaluation of the topic with the congregation. For instance, what do we learn about the Christian attitude toward AIDS and its victims and the Christian responsibility toward AIDS victims? Or what do we learn about baptism that makes a difference in the lives of the listeners and in the corporate life of the church?

Conclusion (5–15 percent). The conclusion gracefully draws the sermon to a close in some way appropriate to the content of the sermon, perhaps by telling a story that embodies the major thrust of the sermon, by summarizing the logic of the sermon, or by raising questions for further consideration.

The strength of the topical sermon is that it makes the whole of life immediately accessible for preaching. The preacher need not twist a text in order to get the text to address some topic that needs discussion in the current milieu. The danger is that the preacher must be solidly grounded theologically in order to render a truly theological interpretation of the topic and not simply to rattle off the latest political, psychological or sociological theory on the topic.

5. The model of thesis-antithesis-synthesis. The sermon based on this model makes maximum use of dissonance in helping the listeners consider the generative theme of the sermon. It can be used with sermons that start from a biblical text as well as with sermons that begin with a topic. The structure and the approximate percentage contribution of each part to the whole sermon follow.

Thesis (30 percent). The preacher describes an interpretation of a text or a topic. Frequently the preacher will summarize the congregation's popular understanding of the text or topic.

Antithesis (30 percent). The preacher honestly criticizes the above interpretation along the lines of appropriateness to the gospel, intelligibility, and moral credibility. This critique will often create a sense of dissonance in the listeners, which will help them be ready for another line of interpretation.

Synthesis (40 percent). This is a constructive phase in which the preacher may draw upon those positive aspects of the thesis and responds to the criticisms of the antithesis in coming to an alternate interpretation. Or, if the preacher has found the thesis altogether wanting, the preacher may simply propose (and explain) a completely different way of approaching the text or subject under discussion. In the synthesis, the preacher engages in the positive aspects of "traditioning" described in the preceding chapter.

This form has the notable advantage of modeling one way of theological thinking. The congregation observes the process of coming to a clear grasp of a position (the thesis) and hears how the preacher wrestles with the position in the light of the gospel (the antithesis). The congregation then joins the preacher in the positive reconstruction of an alternative to the thesis (the synthesis). This model is especially useful when preaching against a text.

6. Innovative sermon forms of the contemporary era. A resurgence of interest in preaching has taken place in the last fifteen years. This resurgence has been fueled, in part, by the awareness that much recent Christian preaching has been dry, uninteresting, and (judging from the health of the churches) lacking in significance to the hearers. Recent homiletical literature locates a part of the problem in dull, noncommunicative sermon forms. This literature widely prescribes new, inventive, more artistic forms for the sermon.

This many-faceted movement calls attention to the importance of several aspects of preaching that have been somewhat neglected in twentieth-century preaching: the importance of the imagination, the power of language as constructing the world of the listener, the distinctive characteristics and strengths of oral discourse, the revelatory power of story, the close connection between the way something is said and what is said, the many different effects of the modes of communication in scripture upon the listener, the insights of contemporary artistic expression (such as drama, cinema, novels, short stories). Such emphases prove remarkably helpful.

Preachers and writers in the field of homiletics, however, sometimes seem to become fascinated with innovative approaches to preaching for the sake of the approaches themselves, almost as if new homiletical technology can itself bring about a renewed pulpit. Yet, we discovered early in our study that the heart of the problem of the historic denominations in this country today lies not simply in outdated or boring *forms* of preaching but in the content of what is preached. Modern listeners sometimes find the *content* of the church's current witness to be insignificant or unintelligible. Thus, while innovation is welcome in the household of homiletics, primary attention must still be paid to the content of the sermon so the sermon bears an adequate witness to the gospel.

Several current approaches to preaching seem to us to offer significant opportunities for bringing form and content together. At the beginning of the new wave of interest in form in preaching, Fred Craddock proposed inductive preaching (Craddock 1971; see now Craddock 1985, 170ff.). Eugene Lowry envisions the sermon as moving in a "loop" through five phases: upsetting the equilibrium of the listener, analyzing the discrepancies, disclosing the clue to resolution, experiencing the gospel, anticipating the consequences. Edmund Steimle, Morris Niedenthal, and Charles Rice see the sermon as moving like a story. David Buttrick, as we have already commented, sees the sermon as a series of moves joined together to form a plot. Thomas G. Long (1989) and Sidney Greidanus show how the literary form of a biblical text can inform the form of preaching from the text (see also Wardlaw).

Every form of Christian preaching teaches. The question that the preacher must answer is this: Does this sermon teach the gospel?

A Plan for Systematic Teaching
from the Pulpit

The individual teaching sermon will have its best effect if it is part of a larger plan of systematic teaching from the pulpit. Of course, each sermon needs to be a self-contained body of meaning for the sake of those who are not in worship every week. But when sermons relate to one another over a period of several weeks, the preacher can deal with a subject in more depth than in only one sermon. (For instance, one can hardly resolve the relationship of suffering and God's love, power, and justice in one twelve-minute slot.) A series of interconnected sermons can have an impressive cumulative effect.

We mention now representative plans whereby preachers can teach systematically from the pulpit.

1. Preaching from a lectionary (based on the principle of lectio selecta) in the context of the Christian year. Most lectionaries in use today are based on the principle of *lectio selecta* (selected reading) in conjunction with the seasons of the Christian year (Advent, Christmas, Epiphany, Lent, Easter, Pentecost). The seasons of the Christian year are intended to remind the congregation of many of the important themes of the Christian faith; the Bible readings are selected because the readings illuminate the themes of the Christian faith that are at the heart of the season. For instance, the Bible readings in Advent are appointed because they help the congregation consider God's coming into the world. The preacher's assignment, then, is to meditate on the concerns of the season in the light of both the text and the events taking place in the life of the community.

A lectionary, when considered in the context of the Christian year, thus gives the preacher an opportunity to think with the congregation in a systematic way (over the course of a year) about some of the important concerns of the Christian faith and to do so with a wide variety of Bible readings. Dan Moseley notices that in its breadth of theological and biblical concern, a lectionary helps protect the preacher from the idolatry of preaching only on her or his favorite texts or themes. Instead, a lectionary leads us away from the tendency to create the Christian tradition in our own provincial images, and it encourages us to consider biblical and theological witnesses that are outside our own special interests. Indeed, preachers frequently express gratitude to the lectionary for designating a text that is very difficult but that causes the preacher to wrestle in a basic (but ultimately rewarding) way with the text and its attendant theological themes.

Even so, the contemporary lectionaries have weaknesses. For instance, in this era when ecological concerns are exceptionally prominent, few lectionaries in use in the churches deal in a systematic way with the doctrine of creation. Again, the lectionaries in use today give disproportionately little attention to the sacred scriptures of Israel. And, the continuous relegation of the sacred scriptures of Israel to the role of supporting the readings from the earliest literature from the hand of the church diminishes the importance of the sacred scriptures of Israel. Furthermore, just as a lectionary can guide one away from idolatry, the lectionary itself can become a golden calf. The preacher can become so enamored of the lectionary that he or she preaches about the assigned text without relating the gospel to the living community. (For assessment of the strengths and weaknesses of the use of lectionaries, see Bailey; Gonzalez and Gonzalez, 38–47; Skudlarek, 45–64; Sanders 1983; Bower, 15–30; Williamson and Allen, 112–115.)

2. Preaching seriatim through a book of the Bible. This plan is sometimes called *lectio continua* (continuous reading) because week by week, the preacher moves through a book of the Bible, passage by passage. The congregation is thus exposed in a systematic way to the content of the book and to the systematic interpretation of the book.

A corollary of the same approach is to preach systematically through a section of a book of the Bible. For example, one might preach through the Joseph cycle in the book of Genesis.

Or, in place of preaching on every pericopae in a biblical book, the preacher could select key passages that illustrate the most important themes of the book. In this way, the preacher could deal with the gist of a book and several of its important pericopae and images in the course of a few weeks.

3. Preaching on an important theme in the Bible or in Christian tradition. Instead of concentrating on a particular text (or series of texts) the preacher might trace a theme through the Bible and into the history of the church in the course of a series of sermons. For example, the preacher might follow the theme of covenant from the stories of creation, to Noah, to Abraham and Sarah, to David, among the prophets, in the literature written by the early church, through the history of the church. What do we learn about the nature of covenant that is instructive to the church of today from these various witnesses?

4. Preaching a series of sermons on foundational Christian doctrines. This approach might be implemented in one of two ways. *(a)* The preacher might preach a series of sermons in which each sermon considers a different aspect of the foundations of the Christian life, for example, a sermon on the nature and activity of God, another on Jesus Christ, another on the Holy Spirit, another on the church, another on the life of the individual Christian. Given the theological illiteracy of the current church, we recommend that such a series be a regular part of the preacher's annual sermon schedule. *(b)* The preacher might explore a single doctrine over a series of several weeks. The doctrine of God, for instance, could be considered in a series, such as: why we believe God exists; what we believe about God's nature and character; how God acts in the world; the difference our knowledge of God makes in the ways in which we live in the world.

5. Preaching a series of sermons on the Christian interpretation of current social or personal phenomena. As in the preceding possibility, the preacher might take one of two approaches. *(a)* The preacher might offer a series in which the preacher considers the Christian interpretation of a different phenomenon each week. The series could begin with an introductory sermon that offers the congregation a model for assessing social and personal phenomena in the light of the gospel and its norms and then move to the systematic consideration of different phenomena, such as apartheid, homelessness, the drug culture, racial injustice, gender discrimination. *(b)* The preacher might offer a series in which each sermon considers a different aspect of a common theme. For example, in a series on understanding sexuality in the light of the gospel, the preacher might focus individual sermons on sexuality in marriage, on sexuality in the gay community, on sexuality among children and youth, on sexuality among single people, on the use of sexual images and allusions in contemporary media.

6. Preaching a series of sermons on questions people ask. The preacher might survey the congregation to give the people an opportunity to say what they would like to hear discussed from the pulpit.

Possible plans for Christian preaching are limited only by the preacher's insight and creativity. Of course, it is important to keep in mind the "big picture" of what is taught from the pulpit over the course of the year. Through the seasons of the church's life, the preacher will want to deal with foundational matters and with matters of size and importance.

Conclusion

The forms of teaching sermons are as various as ministers who preach in a teaching mode. However, all share one common purpose: to teach the gospel. Where the gospel is rightly taught, faith can take root, grow, and blossom. Of course, the teaching sermon cannot bear the full weight of responsibility for a congregation's growth in the gospel. But the teaching sermon can play an important role in helping shape the congregation's theological vision and witness.

6

EVERYTHING TEACHES IN
THE MINISTRY AND IN
THE CHURCH

To this point in the book, we have concentrated on the vocation of the minister as a teacher of the Christian faith. We have argued that the central work of the minister is to be a theologian who reflects critically on the appropriateness, intelligibility, and morality of the Christian witness even while making that witness. In this concluding chapter we make the natural move to suggest that ministers teach in everything they do, and that the church itself teaches both in the manner in which it conducts its internal life and in its witness in the larger community. Everything that happens in ministry and in the church offers people an opportunity to name the world. The question always to be asked is, In everything that we say and do, are we helping people name the world in the terms of the gospel?

At times the act of teaching is quite verbal and explicit, as, for instance, in a classroom setting. At other times the act of teaching may be less verbal but still explicit, as when the minister and the congregation demonstrate through behavior that God graciously loves *all* and seeks justice for *all*.

The church seeks to embody the gospel in all aspects of its own life and in all its forms of mission in the world. Hence, the Christian community will always employ means that are consistent with the gospel: in the act of witnessing to God's love for the world and God's will for justice in the world, the church will itself act in ways that are loving and just.

In this chapter, we begin by offering a vision of the local congregation as a teaching community. By extension, this vision applies to all juridical manifestations of the church. We then consider teaching dimensions in representative aspects of congregational life—worship, pastoral counseling and calling, administration, and program development. We conclude by considering the church as teacher and learner in the world.

The Congregation as Neighborhood
Theological Seminary

One of the emphases in the (relatively) recent studies of language and its importance in human life is the importance of the images that we use to name the world. Images are not merely word-pictures that hang in the gallery of consciousness but are powerful lenses through which we construct the world. Images help us see what is of greater and lesser importance, what is acceptable and unacceptable, what is desirable and undesirable. In so doing, images help us organize our time, energy, and behavior. We act in the world according to the ways in which we see the world.

Therefore, our principal image for the congregation is critically important. For our image of the church will determine how we see the nature and purpose of the church and how we organize the church to carry out its purposes. In a very practical way, a minister's image of the church shapes how the minister spends her or his time and will influence the choice of what things will be supported and what things will be discouraged.

We propose that the congregation is first a neighborhood theological seminary whose primary purpose is to help its members relate the Christian tradition appropriately, intelligibly, and morally to the contemporary world situation and vice versa. The fundamental work of the congregation is to develop Christian consciousness and to provide the congregation with the resources and methods by which to make the Christian witness in the world. Using learning strategies that are appropriate to its constituency, the congregation should do for its members what studies in seminary do for the pastor.

In this vision of the church the raison d'être of the pastor's calling is to see that the congregation provides adequate instruction in the Christian tradition. Broadly speaking, the pastor is the overseer whose goal is to nurture theological consciousness in the congregation so that the congregation will recognize God's presence, power, and purpose in the world and will respond with love, joy, trust, discernment, commitment, and courage.

Edward Farley notes that most congregations have depended largely upon the sermon as the means by which to offer theological instruction to the congregation. However, the sermon by itself is unable to fulfill the responsibility for theological formation in the congregation. Unfortunately, Farley observes, few Christian communities today have significant opportunities for the *"ordered learning"* of the foundations of the Christian faith. That is, few communities are organized so as to introduce members in a careful, systematic way to the Christian tradition and its mutual critical correlation with contemporary life. Learning opportunities in the church today tend to be in the form of Sunday school, in which the focus is largely on the Bible (though seldom on the *critical* interpretation of the Bible) or on a hodgepodge of randomly selected topics. Other opportunities for learning in the church tend to follow in the same vein. What is needed, argues Farley, is a program by which members are systematically and critically introduced to the major elements of the Christian faith (Farley 1988, 85–102).

At the simplest level, then, the congregation can offer a series of classes (and other learning events) that systematically acquaint members and friends with the Christian tradition and with ways both to interpret that tradition for the contemporary world and to interpret the contemporary world in the light of the critically appropriated tradition. The goal of the curriculum is to help the Christian community articulate an appropriate, intelligible, and moral vision of God, the world, God's relationship with the world (the gospel), and the response of the world to God. The church's ordered plan of learning would lead the congregation to love God with all its heart, mind, soul, and strength and to love its neighbors as itself.

We have space to sketch the curriculum only in its broad outlines. The plan might begin by introducing the community to the biblical writings and to the witnesses that those writings made in their own contexts. The program might then move to ways in which the Christian witness was understood before the Enlightenment. The Bible and Christian tradition contain too much material for exhaustive study, but judicious selection of texts, events, themes, and figures can give members a sense of the landscape of the Christian tradition.

The Enlightenment deserves special consideration in the curriculum. More than a pothole in the road of human consciousness, the Enlightenment has caused us to understand the world and consciousness itself fundamentally differently than before. Since the Enlightenment, our ways of understanding the world and our human ways of knowledge have continued to unfold so that today we speak of postenlightenment, postmodern consciousness. Most people in the industrialized world appear to take postenlightenmentism for granted except in the arena of religion. For some, the postenlightenment views of the world seem to make belief in God almost impossible. Hence, while maintaining a basically moral commitment to human relationships, these people abandon religion. Many church people appear not to connect their postenlightenment mentality with religion and end up with religious beliefs that are superstitious, magical, and intellectually pallid, or that reduce the Christian faith to moralism. In short, many church people not only do not know the content and tradition of the Christian faith but do not generally know how to think theologically in the terms of the world in which we live. This may well be an important reason for the church's lack of evangelistic success in the pluralistic setting of North America.

The program of ordered learning would help Christians grasp the best of what we know about the development and functioning of the self and about the human communities in which we live (locally, nationally, globally) as well as about the relationship of the human communities and the natural world. The curriculum would, of course, provide guidance in the practice of the Christian faith in everyday life in such matters as prayer, the Christian's relationships with other persons and with nature, and Christian perspectives on political and social trends.

The pastor (and other supervisors of the curriculum) would continually evaluate its content according to the question, What is necessary for a person to be an optimally functioning Christian today?

The church's program of Christian education would have classes for beginning students and other classes at the intermediate and advanced levels. Learning events could be scheduled at times when the congregation is available (and likely) to come—Sundays or weekdays, weeknights or weekend evenings. Educational methods could be diverse and creative as long as they are consistent with the gospel and enhance learning.

In this view of the church, the minister is first and foremost a teacher. But as the program of ordered learning catches fire, there will be too many opportunities for teaching in the congregation for the pastor to fill them all. Likely, then, the minister will serve as a lead teacher who helps prepare elders and other leaders of the congregation to teach. The pastor is thus an overseer whose responsibility is to see that faithful teaching takes place in the congregation.

Of course, the congregation not only studies the Christian witness but bears Christian testimony in the world. A good program of Christian education will acquaint the community with strategies for making the Christian witness in both individual and corporate ways. Individuals represent the gospel (and the church) in the home and family, in social relationships, through participation in community affairs, in the marketplace. The church itself bears corporate witness in the way in which it relates to the rest of the world, in the positions it takes on public issues, through the program it develops and carries out, by the alliances it makes (and does not make) with other Christian and non-

Christian groups. However, the capacity to bear truthful witness in these arenas depends upon the community's ability to read situations in the light of the gospel.

A good program of ordered learning will provide the church with tools to help evaluate its words and acts of testimony so that the community will be able to constantly assess the appropriateness and effectiveness of its witness.

Worship as Teaching

Scholars in the history, theology, and practice of Christian worship generally agree that the fundamental purpose of Christian worship is to give glory to God (White, 16–22). This is consistent with the biblical traditions in which the basic Hebrew and Greek words translated "to worship" have root meanings of "to serve" and "to prostrate oneself." In the Bible, acts of worship typically have God as their object.

In a similar way, Hughes Oliphant Old sees this emphasis as the basic principle underlying Reformed worship. "One can always find medicine men and gurus who advocate religious rites for the sake of good health, financial success, or peace of mind. True worship, however, is distinguished from these in that it serves above all else the praise of God's glory" (Old, 3). In like fashion, the English word "worship" is derived from a root that denotes "worth ship." The etymology suggests that worship is an act of ascribing worth, with Christian worship being the specific act of declaring the worth of God.

Fundamentally, then, Christian worship is not utilitarian. Its purpose is not first of all raising the church budget or motivating people to attend the Wednesday night fellowship dinner or getting people to vote the right way or proposing solutions to personal or social problems. Worship is an act whose end is to give glory to the living God whose gospel is unconditional love and unbounded justice.

But worship also teaches. Of course, the service contains the teaching moments of the reading of scripture and the sermon. Beyond these, Geoffrey Wainwright notes that worship is "the point at which the whole of the Christian life comes to ritual focus." By ritual, Wainwright means "the descriptive sense of regular patterns of behavior invested with symbolic significance and efficacy" (Wainwright, 8). Thus, a service of worship communicates to the Christian community what is appropriate, intelligible, and moral. Worship does this through the language used in the service, through the leadership of the service, and even through the physical setting in which worship takes place. A key question to ask of every aspect of the service is, What does this teach? Does this service—and each of its parts—teach the gospel?

As we have already noted, language creates our view of the world. Language names the world for us and gives meaning and order to our experience in the world. In this light, language for God is the most important language in the Christian community. The ways we speak of God play a major part in determining how we envision and relate to God. This is especially clear in the names, titles, and descriptions that we use for God. The Christian community conceives of God as unconditional love who wills justice for the whole creation. The teaching that takes place in worship is appropriate to this vision of God when we speak of God in ways that are consistent with one who is pure, unbounded love and who wills for all people and things to be in right relationship with one another. Worship teaches wrongly when it uses language that is not consistent with that vision.

Furthermore, the ways in which we speak of God contribute in a direct way to the ways in which we relate to other persons and communities and to nature. The vision of God is the center of the symbolic universe of the Christian community and it gives the Christian universe its character. We learn how to regard one another and how to relate to the environment by noticing the ways in which God relates to people and to the natural realm. To sing in worship that God is pure unbounded love is to see every person, every opossum, and every rock as beloved of God and to be treated as such. By this, we do not mean that God rejoices with everything that happens in the world (such as the occurrence of cancer in a young woman); we mean that in every situation God is present and God wills the best for all concerned. For example, God is present in suffering love with the cancer victim and God wishes for the cancer itself to lose its destructive power. Thus, love becomes the norm by which to relate to other persons and communities, by which to formulate political views, and by which to set forth environmental and economic policies.

For example, in recent years interpreters have rightly called attention to the language of gender that is used for God. Of course, God has no gender in the creaturely sense, but we sometimes speak of God in metaphors and images that do evoke the characteristics of gender-specific relationships and that apply the characteristics of these relationships to our relationship with God. For instance, to call God "Father" is to say that our relationship with God is similar to the best of our relationships with our human fathers.

But traditional vocabulary for God is predominantly masculine, for example, Father, King, Lord. This preponderance reflects the patriarchal culture that generated these images. But the continued use of predominantly male images for God has the effect of causing the community to transfer its experience of the social roles described by these masculine figures to its experience with God, which, in turn, has the effect of legitimating male dominance in the community and of diminishing the importance of women. Therefore, this aspect of traditional Christian practice teaches an inappropriate understanding of the relationship between women and God and between women and men. Contemporary writers, therefore, see that the church needs to enlarge the vocabulary by which it speaks of God to include metaphors and images that bespeak the experience of women and make extensive use of appropriate relationships that are not associated with gender-specific roles.

Leaders can make a similar analysis of each element of the service of worship. Do the prayers, for instance, reflect the breadth of God's love? When the church prays only for itself, it teaches that those outside the church are not valued either by God or by the Christian community. Do the prayers portray an intelligible understanding of the ways in which God is present within and exercises power in the world?

Do the texts of the hymns voice the actual faith of the church? Do the tunes to which the texts are set create a feeling in the singers that is consistent with the text? Exclusive use of tunes from another era (such as Bach chorales) can intimate that God really belongs only to another era. Excessive use of sentimental texts and tunes can leave the impression that the Christian faith is trite and sentimental. Hymns that are contemporary in theology, imagery, and music teach that God is up-to-date.

Does the Affirmation of Faith (sometimes called a creed) give an accurate account of what the community really believes about the world and God and their interrelationship? Is God's action in the Lord's Supper interpreted intelligibly?

A special problem is posed by the use of materials that come from the history of the church but are inappropriate, unintelligible, or morally offensive. These include some creeds, hymns, prayers, and liturgical practices. The occasional use of such material may have the positive value of helping today's Christian community gain a sense of continuity with generations that have come before. This is no small benefit in late twentieth-century North American culture in which we habitually suffer from historical amnesia. However, the repeated uninterpreted use of such material teaches the congregation that such beliefs, attitudes, and practices are acceptable. Therefore, we suggest adding a teaching moment in the service of worship when difficult material from the past appears in the service or giving an explanation in the bulletin.

The structure of the service has a teaching function as well. Worship brings the Christian life into ritual focus. Like a drama, the service of worship begins, takes us on a journey, brings us to a climax, and concludes. The service thereby becomes a lens through which to view God's purposes for the church and the world. We consider here two examples of structures for worship and what each teaches.

Keith Watkins uses the acronym SRRS to summarize the structure of the emerging ecumenical consensus in worship (Watkins, 15–17). We expand this acronym to SRRRS.

S = Start	The service has a beginning (and an ending). The start of the service establishes the purpose of the service and suggests that the service (and hence, God) is not random or chaotic but purposeful. This part of the service would typically include a call to worship, an opening prayer, and a hymn.
R = Remember	The congregation remembers two things: (1) the brokenness of the world; (2) God's love for the world and God's will for justice in the world. This part of the service would typically include a prayer of confession, Bible readings, and the sermon.
R = Respond	The community responds to the awareness of God's presence with affirmation of faith and the major prayers, especially prayers of intercession. Participation in these liturgical responses indicates the willingness of the congregation to respond to God's love and justice in the whole of life.
R = Renew	God renews the community with the bread and the cup as signs of God's faithfulness and continuing presence with the community.
S = Send Forth	The service of worship stops and the community is sent forth to witness to God's love and will for the whole created order.

The structure of the service teaches that God loves the world even in its brokenness and is ever in the world as loving, redeeming presence. The service teaches that the purpose of the church is to accept God's grace and God's will for justice and to witness to these in all of life.

Another structure for worship that is widely followed in Protestant churches in the United States begins in much the same way as the service just discussed. It then moves to the major prayers, the collection of the offering, the reading of the Bible, and the sermon. The climax of the service is the invitation to discipleship. The order of worship thereby suggests that God wills for all people to become Christian and that the purpose of the church is to serve as an instrument for conversion.

We hasten to add that any structure can be infused with unsuitable (or suitable) theological content. Hence, the ministers and other leaders of worship need constantly to be evaluating the adequacy of the full service.

Worship also teaches through the selection of those who lead services and through the styles with which the leaders lead. The affirmation of the gospel that God loves all is embodied when the leaders of services of worship include the fullness of the human family: women and men, people of various ages, people of different racial and ethnic backgrounds, and people of different economic, social, and educational backgrounds. When the leaders of worship come from a select group within the congregation (such as white, middle-aged, male business leaders), the congregation is taught that these persons are more important to God than others in the community.

Because the gospel is good news, the style with which the leaders lead the service is appropriate when the leaders embody good news by speaking and acting in ways that communicate the quality of good news. When the worship leaders are warm, natural, lively, sincere, and open, they teach the congregation that God is warm, natural, lively, sincere and open. Worship leaders who use an artificial tone of voice, or who speak in monotone, or who move about woodenly teach that God is artificial, dull, and wooden. Indeed, they can teach that we must become other than who we are when we become conscious of God's presence. Since God is always with us, this would mean that we could never be ourselves.

The physical space for worship teaches as well. A sanctuary in which the Lord's Table is distant from the people and in which seating is arranged in regimented, boxlike fashion and in which the people can only see the backs of the heads of other worshipers, has the effect of communicating that God is distant and that the Christian life consists primarily of getting in step with others. However, a center of worship that is near the people and a seating arrangement that allows the people to see one another teaches that God is immediately and intimately present and that the experience of community is integral to the Christian life. A sanctuary that is warm and beautiful and evocative suggests that God and the Christian community are beautiful and warm. A drab, unkept sanctuary implies that God is drab and uncaring.

Gwen Neville and John Westerhoff thus comment, "We humans are made for ritual and, in turn, our rituals make us" (Neville and Westerhoff, 94).

Pastoral Counseling and Calling
as Teaching

The pastoral counseling relationship is typically a one-to-one relationship between the pastor and the counselee. The number of counselees may increase in a single session in the case of family counseling or group counseling, but the number of participants in any counseling session remains small. Pastoral counseling becomes a teaching moment when the pastoral counselor seeks to help the counselee(s) understand the situation and the decisions necessary in the light of the gospel. The counselor hopes the clients will make a critical correlation between the gospel and their life situations and will make decisions and life changes that are appropriate, intelligible, and moral. In the counseling situation the teaching minister functions as a "moral counselor" (Gustafson, 93ff.).

The claim that pastoral counseling is an act of teaching may come as a surprise to some. Indeed, when E. Brooks Holifield traces the history of pastoral care in the United States, he finds that it is a movement from concern with issues related to salvation to helping people achieve self-realization. With respect to pastoral counseling, clergy have grown ever less interested in understanding the counseling relationship in traditional theological categories and ever more committed to understanding the counseling process in purely psychological terms (Holifield). Carl Rogers' client-centered (or nondirective) therapy has been particularly influential. In Rogers' approach, the counselor accepts, without value judgment, everything the client presents. The counselor has unconditional positive regard for the client. The role of the counselor is to mirror to the client the client's responses in the hope that this will activate the innate tendency of the human personality to move toward self-acceptance and even toward transcending those aspects of the nonaccepting culture that are oppressive (Rogers, 481ff.). Although not directly a child of Rogers' theory, the Clinical Pastoral Education movement operates with many of the same emphases.

To be sure, these forces have made very positive contributions to contemporary pastoral counseling. But a principal norm that operates in the counselee's process of coming to self-understanding and decision making is the norm of feeling. An important question is, What feels right? In this context, feeling refers almost altogether to the personal, subjective emotional condition of the client. The key task of the counselor is to help the client identify and accept his or her feelings. The minister gives little attention to the social, moral, and ethical dimensions of the client's life.

Some authorities in the field of pastoral counseling have reacted against the Rogerian model with its individualism, psychological hegemony, and the dominant emphasis on feelings as basis for self-perception and action. Paul Pruyser, for instance, finds that one reason people come to a minister for counseling is that they seek theological interpretation of their situation (Pruyser, 43). In his epic work *The Moral Context of Pastoral Care*, Don Browning argues that proper pastoral care can be given only when the full context of the counselee is taken into account. This context includes the social world of the client and the nexus of moral commitments and values of the client and his or her community. Indeed, conflict between the client and the client's social/moral world is often a source of the client's problem. To conduct therapy without identifying such matters is to ignore a potential source of the problem and a potential resource for help.

In Browning's view, the minister's role in the counseling relationship begins long before the first interview. The minister's role in counseling really begins with the minister's role as a teacher in the Christian community. "The minister has a clear duty to counsel the ill and dying but he should first have helped create a community with a religiocultural view of the meaning of illness and death. Certainly the minister should counsel persons with marriage problems, sexual problems and divorce problems, but he should first have helped create among his people a positive vision of the normative meaning of marriage, sexuality and divorce" (Browning 1976, 108–109).

James Gustafson points to four critical questions that can help client and counselor focus on the moral dimension of the client's situation. (a) What are the full personal, social, meaning-related circumstances in the life situation of the client in which "the ought question comes up"? (b) What are the larger ethical issues in the situation and "what concepts and principles are required to think about them"? (c) Who are the most important moral agents in the situation and "what makes them the sort of moral people they are"? (d) What theological convictions form the framework within which the client and the counselor understand themselves and make practical moral decisions? (Gustafson, 99–100).

The teacher-counselor model does not ask the counselees (or the counselors) to deny or ignore their feelings. Nor does the teacher-counselor act as if Freud and the psychological movement have not taken place. The ministerial counselor certainly does not attempt to speak in an imperial way, telling the client absolutely what the client should think and do. To the contrary, the sensitive pastoral counselor-teacher helps clients explore their feelings and makes full use of the insights of contemporary psychology. The minister does not make (or attempt to force) the important decisions of self-perception and action that only the client can make. But the pastor does try to help the client reflect on these concerns and insights from the perspective of the gospel. When this happens, the counseling session becomes a moment in which the Christian faith is taught.

We cannot present (nor are we qualified to present) a method for counseling in this mode. But it does seem to us that Don Browning offers a practical approach to helping the counseling session become a teaching moment. Browning envisions the counseling relationship as moving in four stages: (1) establishing the relationship between counselor and client and defining the problem; (2) ascertaining the full context of the problem through careful exploration and listening; (3) analyzing the situation critically to determine the fundamental issues involved and comparing different ways in which those issues might be resolved; (4) the making of the client's important decisions and establishing a strategy by which to implement the decisions and assess their effects (Browning 1983a, 51–52, 99–101; Browning 1983b, 187–201).

So far we have concentrated on the formal counseling relationship, which is usually initiated by the parishioner. But the general concern for the one-to-one or one-to-small-group relationship to be considered a teaching moment can be extended to pastoral counseling that occurs in the course of day-to-day pastoral care on such occasions as hospitalization, the death of a loved one, preparation for marriage, change of life situation (such as loss of a job, children leaving home, moving from the family home to a care facility for senior citizens). In each case, the minister seeks to help people name God's presence and purpose in the situation.

This concern can be extended to regular pastoral calling as well. By "regular pastoral calling," we refer to visits to parishioners' homes and places of business that are not occasioned by specific needs and circumstances (such as death, loss of a job) but that take place as a part of the pastor's comprehensive, systematic, planned contact with the membership. Indeed, we think that regular pastoral calling (by the minister and by other leaders of the congregation) has much to teach the congregation.

When the pastor calls only at the time of life disruption, parishioners may subtly assume that God (and the minister and the church) is mainly a crutch for helping people get through tough times. Indeed, the congregation may get the impression that God is passive, waiting in the wings for bad things to happen. Regular pastoral calling teaches by implication that God is present (and interested) in everything that goes on, even in those moments that do not call attention to themselves. In and of itself, the call says, God, the pastor, and the church care about you. A pastoral call on the occasion of joy teaches that God rejoices with us and this knowledge intensifies our own joy. In this way, the pastor carries the gospel from house to house.

Regular pastoral calling also gives the pastor a chance to get a sense of the concerns and interests of the community in the relatively relaxed atmosphere of the home. Sensitive listening can help the pastor get a sense of those areas that need to be addressed through the formal teaching ministry of the church.

Administration and Program Development as Teaching

The pastor has a significant teaching role in the administration of the congregation, especially in helping the congregation conceive and carry out its programs. Administrative occasions (such as the daily management of the church office, board and committee meetings, planning and decision-making processes, recruitment of members for leadership, and participation in church programs) become teaching occasions when the minister—and other leaders in the congregation—help the congregation to evaluate its plans and its programs in the light of the norms of appropriateness, intelligibility, and moral credibility.

Two key questions can be asked of any administrative situation, decision or program. (1) Will this plan or action teach the gospel? (2) Will we implement this plan (in the ways in which we call upon people and utilize resources) in ways that embody the gospel?

The norms of the gospel can be applied systematically to every administrative aspect of the church. But in order for this to happen, the administrative leaders of the congregation need to be schooled in the gospel and in the content and use of the norms. Thus, while the minister may well have important day-to-day administrative responsibilities in the Christian community, the minister's most significant administrative responsibility is to encourage the congregation and its leadership to think theologically about what they are doing and why they are doing it.

One of the key moves in helping the church to think theologically about its life is to help the church remember that its purpose is to witness to the gospel. Many administrative bodies in local congregations (and in middle and upper judicatories as well) seem to operate as if the life of the body is an end in itself. The result is that self-maintenance becomes the functional goal of the body's administrators. Of course, if the church is to continue to be in existence so as to witness to the gospel, the church must give some attention to its own well-being. But institutional survival is never the goal of the church's life.

The purpose of administrators in the church, then, is to reflect on circumstances in the life of the community, to conceive plans and to make decisions that will help the church enact its witness. In the midst of such processes, the pastor is not a political operator who knows how to manipulate the church's machinery and personalities so as to get the church to make the decision she or he wants. The minister is rather the teacher who helps the congregation articulate its vision and translate that vision into day-to-day life. Along the way, the minister is sensitive to those moments in the process that can become teaching moments. Indeed, at such times, the pastor may well interrupt the flow of the decision-making process in order to help the people reflect theologically on what is happening (or not happening).

We now think briefly about how selected aspects of the congregation's administrative life have a teaching function.

We begin with the board of directors (or similar body). The general purpose of the board of directors is to coordinate the everyday work of the church so the gospel is taught through the people selected for leadership, through the church's policies and expenditures, through the programs that are approved and developed. The board of directors thus reflects collectively and theologically on the life of the community. Church members sometimes think that the board of directors conducts the business of the church in the board meeting, but this is not correct. The purpose of the board is to help implement the real business of the church: teaching, worshiping, witnessing.

The congregation learns what is important and unimportant from those matters that the board considers (and does not consider), from the amount of time the board devotes to particular matters, from the decisions the board makes, and from the rationales for the board's decisions. The congregation learns appropriate processes for decision making and appropriate (and inappropriate) Christian attitudes and behaviors from the manner in which the board conducts itself. To take a positive example, the board teaches that God's love is impartial when the board votes to participate wholeheartedly in disaster relief for people in a communist country. To take a negative example, the board teaches that ecological wastefulness is permissible when the board approves the purchase of plastic communion cups that will be used once and then thrown away.

The care and use of the church property provides a particularly visible teaching opportunity. What is taught by the appearance and use of the church grounds and the church building? A building can be well kept, well designed, and can even suggest the presence of transcendence in its grounds and architecture. Such a building intimates that God is caring, beautiful, and present. Or the location, grounds, and design of a church building can be so opulent as to suggest that the church is a country club and that God is a genial, cosmic golf pro whose religion does little more than help humankind improve its swing on a weekend afternoon.

A building that is used by the church and the larger community for concerns of love and justice quietly communicates that God is concerned for these things. A building that is strictly reserved for the congregation alone intimates that God's love is quite conditional: one must become a Christian in order to have access to God's good things. But at the same time, a congregation cannot simply open its doors to all comers. A Klu Klux Klan meeting in a church basement leaves the impression that the church supports the racial attitudes and behaviors represented by the Klan.

Unfortunately, deliberative bodies in the church—and church members generally—often get bogged down in discussion of church property. (This writer remembers a meeting of the board of directors of a student congregation in which one full hour of a bimonthly meeting was devoted to the question of whether to paint the newly installed speed bumps on the parking lot fluorescent green or fluorescent yellow.) This teaches that the property in and of itself is the church's most important concern. The teaching pastor will need to think creatively about how to help the congregation relate in a more fitting manner to the care and use of its property.

The church also teaches in its understanding of stewardship. While financial concerns have generally come under the rubric of stewardship, recent writers in the field of stewardship have rightly stressed that stewardship involves more than money. Douglas John Hall describes Christian existence itself as the stewardship of life in the dominion of death (Hall 1985; see also Hall 1982). In the same vein, another writer proposes that we are "stewards of God's promises to us in the gospel, stewards of God's promised future, God's basileia, stewards of those hopes which God has implanted in us, stewards of the past and its richness, including all those now-forgotten alternatives which were once God's new lures offered to pull God's people forward, stewards of that divine freedom, that discontent that urges us to respond positively to God's promises." Indeed, "we must be stewards of hope" that nuclear holocaust and ecological collapse will not come, that our farmland will not be destroyed, that our cities can become "the city of God," that different kinds of people can learn to live together in mutual support (Williamson 1986, 79; see also Allen 1990). Such a notion of stewardship is appropriate, intelligible, moral, and compelling.

But money is a powerful symbol in our culture. The church teaches in the ways in which it speaks about, and spends, money. Some Christian leaders are reluctant to speak about money. But silence only allows the congregation to think about the Christian relationship to money in whatever terms blow into the unscreened windows of consciousness from sources as diverse as legalistic Christian piety to completely secularized yuppieism.

Even when the church does talk about money for the purpose of encouraging members to underwrite the church budget, the church sometimes teaches inadequate views. For instance, the church sometimes implies that people should give money to the church because that will secure God's love (inappropriate). The church sometimes claims that if people give a lot of money to the church, God will bless them materially (neither appropriate nor intelligible). The church sometimes tries to get people to give to "outreach" by implying that by contributing to outreach offerings the people are supporting bold witnesses overseas when, in fact, most of the outreach offering goes to pay for denominational housekeeping (verging on the immoral). The church sometimes leaves the impression that giving to the church budget is the prime way to give money to God, forgetting that God's concern "is much larger than what we usually call the church and a view of stewardship adequate to it (i.e., God's concern) must include and transcend the church. Our impact on others, including ourselves in the future, is vast; the money I did not send to the United Negro College Fund is just as important as what I sent to the Division of Higher Education (of a particular denomination), perhaps more so" (Williamson 1986, 80).

Further, the congregation makes a teaching statement in the ways it spends its money. The whole of the congregation's expenditures should witness to love and justice. When the congregation spends significant amounts of money for persons and groups who are outside of its immediate fellowship (especially for those who are remarkably different from the church), the church witnesses to God's love for *all* and to God's command for justice for *all*. When the congregation uses money only for itself or for those who mirror it, the church functionally teaches that God's love is for the in group.

The church teaches through its small groups and special programs. Small groups are often organized for the immediate purposes of education, mutual support, mission, or fellowship. But the larger purpose of all small groups is to help people grasp the world in the terms of the gospel in conjunction with others in the group. Small groups are typically formed on the basis of some characteristic common to all participants, such as age, gender, or interest. The group seeks to take advantage of the common experience of the participants in helping the participants think about their situation in the light of the gospel. Some groups will be obviously didactic (perhaps studying a curriculum) while other groups will teach through more indirect means (for instance, through confidential support). But, at some point, the group will want specifically to encourage its members to remember God's presence and purposes. A men's group, for example, can be a point for the gospel to enter into the lives of men. Or, a men's group can be little more than a breakfast club and a source of cheap labor for church fix-it projects.

Staff relationships teach authentic (and inauthentic) ways of relationship in the Christian community. When the senior minister, the associate ministers, the ministers of music, and the clerical staff work together in openness, collegiality, candor, mutual support, and sensitivity to and respect for one another (even when differing), they encourage the congregation to think that the whole of the Christian community should so relate. The opposite is taught when the members of the staff carp at one another, take potshots at each other, take smirking delight at one another's failings, and wear their egos on their sleeves for ease in being bruised. A pastor who rages at the office secretary because of a mistake teaches the congregation that it is permissible to rage at one another.

In addition to coordinating calendars, staff meetings can be regular occasions for theological reflection on the life of the church and for collegial assessments of ministry. This would make the staff meeting a wonderful model for others (groups, households, individuals) in the church.

The Church as Teacher and Learner
in the World

The minister is a teacher in the church. In a similar way, the church is a teacher in the world. Reuel Howe's comment on the relationship among the preacher, the congregation, the sermon, and the world applies to the whole witness of the church. "Preaching . . . is the process by which the preacher and people together bring into being the *church's sermon* as distinct from the preacher's sermon." Those who respond to the preaching within the church bear in themselves the church's sermon, which they share with others "either through spoken word or through action. Only in this way can we carry the sermon beyond the walls of the church" (Howe, 102; our emphasis).

Of course, there is an important difference between the relationship of the minister with the church and that of the church with the world. While each congregation certainly contains a diversity of viewpoints on the Christian faith, the minister can presume a common love for God and a common commitment to respond to God with trust and with lives of faithful discipleship. This common ground cannot be presumed outside the ecclesial community. Current commentators often use the word "pluralistic" to describe the current world community: a potpourri of value systems and approaches to life exist side by side with none acknowledged generally as the authoritative voice. In some settings, differing philosophies live together relatively peacefully while in other settings, different philosophies come into conflict and even result in violence.

How does the church teach in a pluralistic world? The church offers its understanding of life and value to the world, especially trying to help the world to seek to order its life according to the norms of universal love and universal justice. Because the world does not automatically ascribe authority to the church's witness, the church needs to develop internal authority for its witness by showing how its understanding of life makes sense and how it offers genuine hope.

The central conviction of the gospel—that God loves all and seeks justice for all—directly informs the character of the church's teaching relationship with the world. God's love for all means that those to whom the church offers its understanding of life are already God's beloved (whether they know it or care about it) and are to be regarded and treated as such. Therefore, the church approaches those outside of its fellowship not as objects at whom to shoot gospel bullets but as genuine others whom we already love because we know them to be loved by God.

A general theological awareness also informs the character of the church's teaching relationship with the world. The church, because it is a created thing, is temporal and relative and is not transcendent and absolute. While the church rightly has confidence in God and the gospel, the temporality of the church means that the church cannot claim to have an exhaustive and unquestionable hold on truth. Like all good teachers, the church continues to learn, and it can learn from the very culture in which it bears witness.

At the simplest level, the church learns how the world understands and talks about itself so that the church can adequately correlate the gospel with the experience of the world. The church needs to know those with whom it speaks as the people they really are. The church is immoral when it speaks of caricatures and straw people.

But at a deeper level, when the church enters into dialogue with the world, the church exposes its witness to the questions and assessments of the world. In so doing, the church may find that the questions and criticisms of others cause the church to reevaluate aspects of its witness. Thus, as the church learns from the world, the church engages in mutual critical correlation: the church correlates its witness with the situation and insights of the world even while the world causes the church to rethink its witness. As noted earlier in the volume, the witness of the church may thus be transformed.

The church as teacher in the world is less like the droning lecturer reading tired notes off a yellowed page than it is like a participant in a seminar. The seminar participant arrives at the table with a position and with ideas and convictions but is committed to joining in exciting conversation that is marked by provocative questions, challenges to assess and reassess the position and its supporting data, and flashes of insight and of discovering fresh importance in old and taken-for-granted conclusions. In the process of exploration, the participants often discover commonalities of which they were previously unaware and are able to see differences in fresh ways.

The question that haunts the church is the degree to which the essence of the gospel might be compromised through such encounters. But at just this juncture, the church can take heart in the confidence that the gospel is God's. God can be trusted not to let the light of the gospel fade out altogether. In any case, if the church is to err, it is better to err on the side of generosity than of small-mindedness.

From time to time, crises arise when there is little time for conversation and when the church, in order to make a witness, must act quickly to say yes! or no! Even so, the church makes its witness with the humility born of the knowledge that its judgments are not absolute. The church should subsequently reflect upon its judgments in a wide community of discourse.

Conclusion

Neil Postman notes that teaching is a two-pronged enterprise. On the one hand, it is a subversive activity (Postman and Weingartner 1969). Indeed, "teaching is by nature a disturbing activity. It tests and questions people. It elicits responses from them that alter perceptions, change courses of action, and require hard decisions. Teachers confront people with their finitude. They point to their bondage. They identify the sources of their security and they question their idolatries." To be sure, "these actions require risk, challenge and courage of the teachers" (Foster, 121).

On the other hand, Postman rightly sees teaching as a conserving activity. Postman's words, written about the education of children, can be read as applying to the church. "The major role of education in the years immediately ahead is to help conserve that which is both necessary to a human survival and threatened by a furious and exhausting culture" (Postman 1979, 25).

The teaching of the gospel does subvert the human penchant for making absolute the transient and the relative. But the teaching of the gospel also conserves that which calms a furious and exhausting culture. Thus, we can hardly do better today than to speak of the minister as a teacher of the Christian faith and to think of the church as itself a teaching community.

WORKS CITED

Allen, Ronald J. 1990. "Partnership as a Metaphor for Preaching on Steward-ship." In *Preaching In and Out of Season*, ed. Thomas G. Long and Neely Dixon McCarter. Louisville, Ky.: Westminster/John Knox Press.

Anderson, Bernard. 1986. *Understanding the Old Testament.* 4th ed. Englewood Cliffs, N.J.: Prentice-Hall.

Augustine, St. 1958. *On Christian Doctrine,* tr. D. W. Robertson, Jr. Indianapolis: Bobbs-Merrill Co.

Aune, David. 1983. *Prophecy in Early Christianity.* Grand Rapids: Wm. B. Eerdmans Publishing Co.

———. 1987. *The New Testament in Its Literary Environment.* Philadelphia: Westminster Press.

Bailey, Lloyd. 1977. "The Lectionary in Critical Perspective," *Interpretation* 31:139–153.

Bainton, Roland H. 1956. "The Ministry in the Middle Ages." In *The Ministry in Historical Perspectives*, ed. H. Richard Niebuhr and Daniel D. Williams. New York: Harper & Brothers: 82–109.

Barth, Karl. 1936. *The Doctrine of the Word of God, Church Dogmatics*, vol. 1 part 1, tr. G. T. Thomson. Edinburgh: T. & T. Clark.

Bartlett, David. 1977. *Paul's Vision for the Teaching Church.* Valley Forge, Pa.: Judson Press.

Bass, Dorothy C. 1989. "Reflections on the Reports of Decline in Mainstream Protestantism." *The Chicago Theological Seminary Register* LXXX:5–15.

Baxter, Richard. 1956. *The Reformed Pastor*, ed. Hugh Martin. London: SCM Press.

Bellah, Robert N., et al. 1985. *Habits of the Heart.* Berkeley, Calif.: University of California Press.

Berger, Peter L. 1986. "American Religion: Conservative Upsurge, Liberal Prospects." In *Liberal Protestantism: Realities and Possibilities*, ed. Robert S. Michaelsen and Wade Clark Roof. New York: Pilgrim Press: 19–36.

Berger, Peter L., and Thomas Luckmann. 1966. *The Social Construction of Reality.* Garden City, N.Y.: Doubleday & Co.

Beyer, Hermann. 1964. "episkeptomai." *Theological Dictionary of the New Testa-*

ment, vol. 2, ed. Gerhard Kittel, tr. Geoffrey Bromiley. Grand Rapids: Wm. B. Eerdmans Publishing Co.: 599–621.

Black, C. Clifton. 1988. "The Rhetorical Form of the Hellenistic Jewish and Early Christian Sermon: A Response to Lawrence Wills." *Harvard Theological Review* 81:1–18.

Blackwood, Andrew. 1948. *The Preparation of Sermons*. Nashville: Abingdon Press.

Blaisdell, Charles. 1986. "Beyond the Profession of Ministry." *Encounter* 47:41–60.

Borgen, Peder. 1965. *Bread from Heaven*. Leiden: E. J. Brill.

Boring, M. Eugene. 1982. *Sayings of the Risen Jesus*. Cambridge: Cambridge University Press.

Bornkamm, G. 1968. "presbus." *Theological Dictionary of the New Testament*, vol. 4, ed. G. Friedrich and G. Kittel, tr. G. Bromiley. Grand Rapids: Wm. B. Eerdmans Publishing Co.: 651–682.

Bower, Peter C. 1987. *Handbook for the Common Lectionary*. Philadelphia: Geneva Press.

Brown, Raymond E. 1966. *The Gospel According to John I–XII*. Garden City, N.Y.: Doubleday & Co.

———. 1970. *The Gospel According to John XIII–XXI*. Garden City, N.Y.: Doubleday & Co.

———. 1979. *The Community of the Beloved Disciple*. New York: Paulist Press.

———. 1984. *The Churches the Apostles Left Behind*. Ramsey, N.J.: Paulist Press.

Browning, Don S. 1976. *The Moral Context of Pastoral Care*. Philadelphia: Fortress Press.

———. 1983a. *Religious Ethics and Pastoral Care*. Philadelphia: Fortress Press.

———. 1983b. "Pastoral Theology in a Pluralistic Age." In *Practical Theology*, ed. Don S. Browning. San Francisco: Harper & Row: 186–202.

Buttrick, David G. 1987. *Homiletic*. Philadelphia: Fortress Press.

Calvin, John. 1960. *Institutes of the Christian Religion*, vol. 2, ed. J. T. McNeill, tr. Ford Lewis Battles. Philadelphia: Westminster Press.

Charlesworth, James, ed. 1983. *The Old Testament Pseudepigrapha*, vol. 1. Garden City, N.Y.: Doubleday & Co.

———. 1985. *The Old Testament Pseudepigrapha*, vol. 2. Garden City, N.Y.: Doubleday & Co.

Childs, Brevard. 1962. *Memory and Tradition in Israel*. London: SCM Press.

Chrysostom, John. 1964. *Six Books on the Priesthood*, ed. Graham Neville. London: SPCK.

Clements, Ronald. 1969. *God's Chosen People*. Valley Forge, Pa: Judson Press.

Cohen, Shaye. 1987. *From the Maccabees to the Mishnah*. Philadelphia: Westminster Press.

Conzelmann, Hans. 1975. *First Corinthians*, tr. James Leitch. Philadelphia: Fortress Press.

Cope, O. Lamar. 1976. *Matthew: A Scribe Trained for the Kingdom of Heaven*. Washington, D.C.: Catholic Biblical Association of America.

Cox, James W. 1985. *Preaching*. San Francisco: Harper & Row.

Craddock, Fred. 1971. *As One Without Authority*. Nashville: Abingdon Press.

———. 1978. *Overhearing the Gospel*. Nashville: Abingdon Press.

———. 1982. *John*. Atlanta: John Knox Press.

———. 1985. *Preaching*. Nashville: Abingdon Press.

Craigie, Peter C. 1976. *The Book of Deuteronomy*. Sevenoaks, Kent: Hodder & Stoughton.

Crenshaw, James. 1981. *Old Testament Wisdom*. Atlanta: John Knox Press.

———. 1985. "Education in Ancient Israel." *Journal of Biblical Literature* 104:601–615.

Dahl, Nils. 1976. *Jesus in the Memory of the Church*. Minneapolis: Augsburg Publishing House.

Davies, W. D. 1955. *Paul and Rabbinic Judaism*, rev. ed. London: SPCK.

Davis, H. Grady. 1958. *Design for Preaching*. Philadelphia: Fortress Press.

Deanesly, Margaret. 1957. *A History of the Medieval Church, 590–1500*. London: Methuen & Co.

Derr, Thomas Sieger. 1988. "Continuity and Change in Mainline Protestantism." In *The Believable Futures of American Protestantism*, ed. Richard John Neuhaus. Grand Rapids: Wm. B. Eerdmans Publishing Co.: 49–71.

Dibelius, Martin, and Hans Conzelmann. 1972. *The Pastoral Epistles*, tr. Philip Buttolph and Adelea Yarbro. Philadelphia: Fortress Press.

Dodd, C. H. 1944. *The Apostolic Preaching and Its Developments*. London: Hodder & Stoughton.

Doeve, J. W. 1954. *Jewish Hermeneutics in the Synoptic Gospels and Acts*. Assen, Netherlands: Koningkluke Van Gorcum.

Donfried, Karl Paul. 1974. *The Setting of Second Clement in Early Christianity*. Leiden: E. J. Brill.

Dunn, James. 1975. *Jesus and the Spirit*. Philadelphia: Westminster Press.

Eliot, T. S. 1933. *After Strange Gods*. New York: Harcourt, Brace & Co.

Epstein, I., tr. 1938. "Shabbath." In *The Babylonian Talmud*. London: Soncino.

Fallaw, Wesner. 1960. *Church Education for Tomorrow*. Philadelphia: Westminster Press.

Farley, Edward. 1983. *Theologia*. Philadelphia: Fortress Press.

———. 1988. *The Fragility of Knowledge*. Philadelphia: Fortress Press.

Fiorenza, Elisabeth S., ed. 1976. *Aspects of Religious Propaganda in Judaism and Early Christianity*. Notre Dame, Ind.: University of Notre Dame.

Fitzmyer, Joseph. 1981. *The Gospel According to Luke I–IX*. Garden City, N.Y.: Doubleday & Co.

———. 1985. *The Gospel According to Luke X–XXIV*. Garden City, N.Y.: Doubleday & Co.

Foster, Charles. 1982. *Teaching in the Community of Faith*. Nashville: Abingdon Press.

Frend, W. H. C. 1984. *The Rise of Christianity*. Philadelphia: Fortress Press.

Friedrich, Gerhard. 1964. "euangelizomai." *Theological Dictionary of the New Testament*, vol. 2, ed. Gerhard Kittel, tr. Geoffrey Bromiley. Grand Rapids: Wm. B. Eerdmans Publishing Co.: 707–737.

———. 1965. "kerux." *Theological Dictionary of the New Testament*, vol. 3, ed. Gerhard Kittel, tr. Geoffrey Bromiley. Grand Rapids: Wm. B. Eerdmans Publishing Co.: 673–718.

Furnish, Victor. 1968. *Theology and Ethics in Paul*. Nashville: Abingdon Press.

Gager, John G. 1975. *Kingdom and Community*. Englewood Cliffs, N.J.: Prentice-Hall.

Gaustad, Edwin S. 1986. "Our Country: One Century Later." In *Liberal Protestantism*, ed. Robert S. Michaelsen and Wade Clark Roof. New York: Pilgrim Press: 85–101.

Geertz, Clifford. 1973. *The Interpretation of Cultures: Selected Essays*. New York: Basic Books.

Georgi, Dieter. 1986. *The Opponents of Paul in Second Corinthians*, tr. Harold Attridge, et al. Philadelphia: Fortress Press.

Gilkey, Langdon. 1964. *How the Church Can Minister to the World Without Losing Itself*. New York: Harper & Row.

Gonzalez, Justo, and Catherine Gonzalez. 1980. *Liberation Preaching*. Nashville: Abingdon Press.

Goodykoontz, Harry G. 1963. *The Minister in the Reformed Tradition*. Richmond: John Knox Press.

Grassi, Joseph. 1982. *Teaching the Way*. Lanham, Md.: University Press of America.

Greeven, Heinrich. 1952. "Propheten, Lehrer, Vorsteher bei Paulus." *Zeitschrift für die neutestamentliche Wissenschaft* 44:1–43.

Gregory the Great. 1956. *The Book of Pastoral Rule*, tr. James Barmby. *The Nicene and Post-Nicene Fathers*, 2d series, vol. 12:1–72.

Gregory of Nazianzus. 1956. "In Defence of His Flight to Pontus," tr. C. G. Browne and J. E. Swallow. *The Nicene and Post-Nicene Fathers*, 2d series, vol. 7:204–227.

Greidanus, Sidney. 1988. *The Modern Preacher and the Ancient Text*. Grand Rapids: Wm. B. Eerdmans Publishing Co.

Gustafson, James. 1988. "The Minister as Moral Counselor." In *The Church and Pastoral Care*, ed. Leroy Aden and J. Harold Ellens. Grand Rapids: Baker Book House: 93–102.

Hadden, Jeffrey K. 1969. *The Gathering Storm in the Churches*. Garden City, N.Y.: Doubleday & Co.

Hall, Douglas John. 1982. *The Steward: Biblical Symbol Come of Age*. New York: Friendship Press.

————1985. *The Stewardship of Life in the Kingdom of Death*. New York: Friendship Press.

Hammond, Phillip E. 1986. "The Extravasation of the Sacred and the Crisis in Liberal Protestantism." In *Liberal Protestantism*, ed. Robert S. Michaelsen and Wade Clark Roof. New York: Pilgrim Press: 51–64.

Hardy, Edward Rochie, Jr. 1956. "Priestly Ministries in the Modern Church." In *The Ministry in Historical Perspectives*, ed. H. Richard Niebuhr and Daniel Day Williams. New York: Harper & Brothers: 149–179.

Harris, Maria. 1987. *Teaching and Religious Imagination*. San Francisco: Harper & Row.

Heinemann, Joseph. 1971. "Preaching." In *Encyclopaedia Judaica*, vol. 13. New York: Macmillan Co.: 994–998.

Held, H. J. 1963. "Matthew as Interpreter of the Miracle Stories." In *Tradition and*

Interpretation in Matthew, ed. Guenther Bornkamm, Gerhard Barth, and Heinze Joachim Held, tr. Percy Scott. Philadelphia: Westminster Press, 165–295.

Henderson, Robert W. 1962. *The Teaching Office in the Reformed Tradition*. Philadelphia: Westminster Press.

Hengel, Martin. 1974. *Judaism and Hellenism*, tr. John Bowden. Philadelphia: Fortress Press.

Hill, David. 1977. "Christian Prophets as Teachers or Instructors in the Church." In *Prophetic Vocation in the New Testament and Today*, ed. J. Panagopoulos. Leiden: E. J. Brill: 108–129.

———. 1979. *New Testament Prophecy*. Atlanta: John Knox Press.

Holifield, E. Brooks. 1983. *A History of Pastoral Care in America*. Nashville: Abingdon Press.

Hough, Joseph C., Jr., and John B. Cobb, Jr. 1985. *Christian Identity and Theological Education*. Decatur, Ga.: Scholars Press.

Howe, Reuel L. 1967. *Partners in Preaching*. New York: Seabury Press.

Hudson, Winthrop S. 1956. "The Ministry in the Puritan Age." In *The Ministry in Historical Perspectives*, ed. H. Richard Niebuhr and Daniel D. Williams. New York: Harper & Brothers: 180–206.

Hunter, James Davison. 1988. "American Protestantism: Sorting Out the Present, Looking Toward the Future." In *The Believable Futures of American Protestantism*, ed. Richard John Neuhaus. Grand Rapids: Wm. B. Eerdmans Publishing Co.: 18–46.

Irenaeus. 1975. *Against the Heresies*, III, Preface—4.2, tr. E. R. Hardy. In *Documents in Early Christian Thought*, ed. Maurice Wiles and Mark Santer. Cambridge: Cambridge University Press: 128–132.

Jenkins, Daniel T. 1947. *The Gift of Ministry*. London: Faber & Faber.

Jensen, Richard. 1980. *Telling the Story*. Minneapolis: Augsburg Publishing House.

Johnson, Benton. 1986. "Winning Lost Sheep: A Recovery Course for Liberal Protestantism." In *Liberal Protestantism: Realities and Possibilities*, ed. Robert S. Michaelsen and Wade Clark Roof. New York: Pilgrim Press: 220–234.

Johnson, Luke T. 1983. *Decision Making in the Bible*. Philadelphia: Fortress Press.

———. 1986. *The Writings of the New Testament*. Philadelphia: Fortress Press.

Kavanaugh, Aiden. 1974. "Teaching Through Liturgy." *Notre Dame Journal of Education* 5:35–47.

Kelley, Dean M. 1972. *Why Conservative Churches Are Growing*. New York: Harper & Row.

Kingsbury, Jack. 1986. *Matthew: Proclamation Commentaries*, rev. ed. Philadelphia: Fortress Press.

Knox, John. 1956. "The Ministry in the Primitive Church." In *The Ministry in Historical Perspectives*, ed. H. Richard Niebuhr and Daniel D. Williams. New York: Harper & Brothers: 1–26.

Koester, Helmut. 1982. *Introduction to the New Testament*, vol. 1. Philadelphia: Fortress Press.

Lapide, Pinchas. 1982. *The Sermon on the Mount*. Maryknoll, N.Y.: Orbis Books.

Leith, John H. 1988. *The Reformed Imperative: What the Church Has to Say That No One Else Can Say*. Philadelphia: Westminster Press.

Lohse, Eduard. 1968. "rabbi." *Theological Dictionary of the New Testament*, vol. 6, ed. Gerhard Kittel and Gerhard Friedrich; tr. Geoffrey Bromiley. Grand Rapids: Wm. B. Eerdmans Publishing Co.: 961–965.

Long, Thomas G. 1988. *The Senses of Preaching*. Atlanta: John Knox Press.

———. 1989. *Preaching and the Literary Forms of the Bible*. Philadelphia: Fortress Press.

Lowry, Eugene. 1980. *The Homiletical Plot*. Atlanta: John Knox Press.

Marrou, H. I. 1956. *A History of Education in Antiquity*, tr. George Lamb. New York: Sheed & Ward.

Marty, Martin E. 1973. *The Fire We Can Light*. Garden City, N.Y.: Doubleday & Co.

Martyn, J. Louis. 1979. *History and Theology in the Fourth Gospel*, rev. ed. Nashville: Abingdon Press.

McKinney, William, and Wade Clark Roof. 1986. "Liberal Protestantism: A Sociodemographic Perspective." In *Liberal Protestantism: Realities and Possibilities*, ed. Robert S. Michaelsen and Wade Clark Roof. New York: Pilgrim Press: 37–50.

———. 1987. *American Mainline Religion*. New Brunswick, N.J.: Rutgers University Press.

Meeks, Wayne A. 1983. *The First Urban Christians*. New Haven, Conn.: Yale University Press.

Michaelsen, Robert S. 1956. "The Protestant Ministry in America: 1850 to the Present." In *The Ministry in Historical Perspectives*, ed. H. Richard Niebuhr and Daniel D. Williams. New York: Harper & Brothers: 250–288.

Minear, Paul. 1976. *To Heal and to Reveal*. New York: Seabury Press.

Minucius Felix. 1979. *The Octavius*, tr. R. E. Wallis. *The Ante-Nicene Fathers*, vol. 4. Grand Rapids: Wm. B. Eerdmans Publishing Co.: 171–198.

Moore, George Foot. 1927. *Judaism*, vol. 1. Cambridge, Mass.: Harvard University Press.

Moseley, Dan P. 1989. "Lectionary: Guard Against Heresy." *Biblical Preaching Journal* 2 (1):46.

Mounce, Robert. 1960. *The Essential Nature of New Testament Preaching*. Grand Rapids: Wm. B. Eerdmans Publishing Co.

Neuhaus, Richard John, ed. 1988. *The Believable Futures of American Protestantism*. Grand Rapids: Wm. B. Eerdmans Publishing Co.

Neusner, Jacob. 1979. *From Politics to Piety*. New York: KTAV Publishing House.

———. 1983. *Midrash in Context*. Philadelphia: Fortress Press.

———. 1987. *What Is Midrash?* Philadelphia: Fortress Press.

———. 1989. *Invitation to Midrash*. San Francisco: Harper & Row.

Neville, Gwen, and John Westerhoff. 1978. *Learning Through Liturgy*. New York: Seabury Press.

Niebuhr, H. Richard, with Daniel D. Williams and James W. Gustafson. 1956. *The Purpose of the Church and Its Ministry*. New York: Harper & Brothers.

Oden, Thomas C. 1988. "Toward a Theologically Informed Renewal of American Protestantism: Propositions for Debate Attested by Classical Arguments." In *The Believable Futures of American Protestantism*, ed. Richard John Neuhaus. Grand Rapids: Wm. B. Eerdmans Publishing Co.: 72–102.

Ogden, Schubert M. 1982. *The Point of Christology*. New York: Harper & Row.

———. 1986. *On Theology*. San Francisco: Harper & Row.

Old, Hughes Oliphant. 1984. *Worship: Guides to the Reformed Tradition.* Atlanta: John Knox Press.

Origen. 1975. *On First Principles,* IV, 2, 1–9. In *Documents in Early Christian Thought,* ed. M. Wiles and M. Santer. Cambridge: Cambridge University Press: 138–145.

Osmer, Richard. 1989. "The Teaching Offices of the Church: The Contribution of Luther and Calvin." Unpublished paper.

Pauck, Wilhelm. 1956. "The Ministry in the Time of the Continental Reformation." In *The Ministry in Historical Perspectives,* ed. H. Richard Niebuhr and Daniel D. Williams. New York: Harper & Brothers: 110–148.

Placher, William C. 1989. *Unapologetic Theology: A Christian Voice in a Pluralistic Conversation.* Louisville, Ky.: Westminster/John Knox Press.

Polzin, Robert. 1980. *Moses and the Deuteronomist.* New York: Seabury Press.

Postman, Neil. 1979. *Teaching as a Conserving Activity.* New York: Delacorte.

Postman, Neil, and Charles Weingartner. 1969. *Teaching as a Subversive Activity.* New York: Dell Publishing Co.

Pruyser, Paul. 1976. *The Minister as Diagnostician.* Philadelphia: Westminster Press.

Rabinowitz, Louis R. 1971. "Synagogue." In *Encyclopaedia Judaica,* vol. 15. New York: Macmillan Publishing Co.: 579–583.

Reicke, Bo. 1953. "A Synopsis of Early Christian Preaching." In *Root of the Vine,* ed. Anton Fridrichsen. New York: Philosophical Library: 126–160.

Rengstorf, Karl H. 1964. "didasko." *Theological Dictionary of the New Testament,* vol. 2, ed. Gerhard Kittel, tr. Geoffrey Bromiley. Grand Rapids: Wm. B. Eerdmans Publishing Co.: 135–165.

Rhoads, David, and Donald Michie. 1982. *Mark as Story.* Philadelphia: Fortress Press.

Rieff, Philip. 1966. *The Triumph of the Therapeutic.* Chicago: University of Chicago Press.

Rivkin, Ellis. 1978. *A Hidden Revolution.* Nashville: Abingdon Press.

Robbins, Vernon. 1984. *Jesus the Teacher.* Philadelphia: Fortress Press.

Roberts, D. Bruce. 1988. "Theological Education and Field Education: A Parallel Process." Unpublished paper.

Roetzel, Calvin. 1985. *The World That Shaped the New Testament.* Atlanta: John Knox Press.

Rogers, Carl. 1961. *On Becoming a Person.* Boston: Houghton Mifflin Co.

Sanders, E. P. 1977. *Paul and Palestinian Judaism.* Philadelphia: Fortress Press.

———. 1985. *Jesus and Judaism.* Philadelphia: Fortress Press.

Sanders, James A. 1972. *Torah and Canon.* Philadelphia: Fortress Press.

———. 1983. "Canon and Calendar: An Alternative Lectionary Proposal." In *Social Themes of the Christian Year,* ed. Dieter Hessel. Philadelphia: Geneva Press: 257–263.

———. 1984. *Canon and Community.* Philadelphia: Fortress Press.

Schechter, Solomon. 1961. *Aspects of Rabbinic Theology.* New York: Schocken Books.

Schrage, Wolfgang. 1971. "synagogue." *Theological Dictionary of the New Testa-*

ment, vol. 7, ed. Gerhard Kittel and Gerhard Friedrich; tr. Geoffrey Bromiley. Grand Rapids: Wm. B. Eerdmans Publishing Co.: 798–851.

Sigal, Phillip. 1986. *The Halakah of Jesus of Nazareth According to the Gospel of Matthew*. Lanham, Md.: University Press of America.

Simmons, John K. 1986. "Complementism: Liberal Protestantism Potential Within a Fully Realized Pluralistic Cultural Environment." In *Liberal Protestantism: Realities and Possibilities*, ed. Robert S. Michaelsen and Wade Clark Roof. New York: Pilgrim Press: 167–197.

Skudlarek, William. 1981. *The Word in Worship*. Nashville: Abingdon Press.

Smart, James D. 1954. *The Teaching Ministry of the Church*. Philadelphia: Westminster Press.

———. 1960. *Rebirth of Ministry*. Philadelphia: Westminster Press.

Smith, Timothy L. 1988. "Evangelical Christianity and American Culture." In *The Believable Futures of American Protestantism*, ed. Richard John Neuhaus. Grand Rapids: Wm. B. Eerdmans Publishing Co.: 1–17.

Stallsworth, Paul T. 1988. "The Story of an Encounter." In *The Believable Futures of American Protestantism*, ed. Richard John Neuhaus. Grand Rapids: Wm. B. Eerdmans Publishing Co.: 103–150.

Steimle, Edmund, Morris Niedenthal, and Charles Rice. 1980. *Preaching the Story*. Philadelphia: Fortress Press.

Stendahl, Krister. 1968. *The School of St. Matthew*. Philadelphia: Fortress Press.

Stowers, Stanley. 1981. *The Diatribe and Paul's Letter to the Romans*. Chico, Calif.: Scholars Press.

Talbert, Charles. 1970. "The Redaction Critical Quest for Luke the Theologian." In *Jesus and Man's Hope*, ed. David G. Buttrick. Pittsburgh: Pittsburgh Theological Seminary: 171–222.

———. 1982. *Reading Luke*. New York: Crossroad.

Tcherikover, Victor. 1959. *Hellenistic Civilization and the Jews*, tr. S. Applebaum. Philadelphia: Jewish Publication Society of America.

Tracy, David. 1975. *Blessed Rage for Order: The New Pluralism in Theology*. New York: Seabury Press.

———. 1985. "Theological Method." In *Christian Theology: An Introduction to Its Traditions and Tasks*, ed. Peter C. Hodgson and Robert H. King. Philadelphia: Fortress Press: 35–60.

———. 1987. *Plurality and Ambiguity*. San Francisco: Harper & Row.

van Buren, Paul M. 1988. *Christ in Context*. New York: Harper & Row.

Vermes, Geza. 1961. *Scripture and Tradition in Judaism*. Leiden: E. J. Brill.

von Campenhausen, Hans. 1969. *Ecclesiastical Authority and Spiritual Power*, tr. J. A. Baker. Stanford, Calif.: Stanford University Press.

von Rad, Gerhard. 1953. *Studies in Deuteronomy*, tr. David Stalker. London: SCM Press.

———. 1966. *The Problem of the Hexateuch and Other Essays*, tr. E. W. Dicken. New York: McGraw-Hill Book Co.

———. 1972. *Wisdom in Israel*. Nashville: Abingdon Press.

Wainwright, Geoffrey. 1980. *Doxology*. New York: Oxford University Press.

Wardlaw, Don M., ed. 1983. *Preaching Biblically*. Philadelphia: Westminster Press.

Watkins, Keith. 1981. *Leader of Word and Sacrament*. Indianapolis: Christian Theological Seminary Bookstore.

White, James. 1980. *Introduction to Christian Worship*. Nashville: Abingdon Press.

Whitehead, Alfred North. 1926. *Religion in the Making*. New York: Macmillan Publishing Co.

———. 1979. *Process and Reality*, corrected ed., ed. David R. Griffin and Donald W. Sherburne. New York: Free Press.

Williams, Donald M. 1967. *The Imitation of Christ in Paul with Special Reference to Paul as Teacher*. Unpublished Ph.D. dissertation. New York: Columbia University.

Williams, George H. 1956a. "The Ministry of the Ante-Nicene Church." In *The Ministry in Historical Perspectives*, ed. H. Richard Niebuhr and Daniel D. Williams. New York: Harper & Brothers: 27–59.

———. 1956b. "The Ministry in the Later Patristic Period." In *The Ministry in Historical Perspectives*, ed. H. Richard Niebuhr and Daniel D. Williams. New York: Harper & Brothers: 60–81.

Williamson, Clark M. 1986. "Good Stewards of God's Varied Grace." *Encounter* 47:61–84.

Williamson, Clark M., and Ronald J. Allen. 1989. *Interpreting Difficult Texts*. London: SCM Press and Philadelphia: Trinity Press International.

Willimon, William. 1979. *Worship as Pastoral Care*. Nashville: Abingdon Press.

Wills, Lawrence. 1984. "The Form of the Sermon in Hellenistic Judaism and Early Christianity." *Harvard Theological Review* 77:277–299.

Worley, Robert C. 1967. *Preaching and Teaching in the Earliest Church*. Philadelphia: Westminster Press.

Wuthnow, Robert. 1988. *The Restructuring of American Religion*. Princeton, N.J.: Princeton University Press.

Zikmund, Barbara Brown. 1986. "Liberal Protestantism and the Language of Faith." In *Liberal Protestantism: Realities and Possibilities*, ed. Robert S. Michaelsen and Wade Clark Roof. New York: Pilgrim Press: 183–197.

INDEX

87 15 chars of teachg sermon
117 most imp prt of admn